WANDERING MOTHER

AN INSPIRATIONAL FICTION NOVEL
PATH TO FAMILY BOOK 2

WRITTEN BY
LEIGH LiNCOLN

MW01247008

© 2024 ALL RIGHTS RESERVED.

Published by She Rises Studios Publishing **www.SheRisesStudios.com**

No part of this book may be reproduced or transmitted in any form whatsoever, electronic, or mechanical, including photocopying, recording, or by any informational storage or retrieval system without the expressed written, dated and signed permission from the publisher and author.

LIMITS OF LIABILITY/DISCLAIMER OF WARRANTY:

The author and publisher of this book have used their best efforts in preparing this material. While every attempt has been made to verify the information provided in this book, neither the author nor the publisher assumes any responsibility for any errors, omissions, or inaccuracies.

The author and publisher make no representation or warranties with respect to the accuracy, applicability, or completeness of the contents of this book. They disclaim any warranties (expressed or implied), merchantability, or for any purpose. The author and publisher shall in no event be held liable for any loss or other damages, including but not limited to special, incidental, consequential, or other damages.

ISBN: 978-1-964619-48-4

Table of Contents

CHAPTER 1

New Mexico – Present Day

"She called again." Stan's loud huff echoed over the line. "She said to make sure to tell you about the green outfit. Whatever that means. So Donna, are you ready to tell me the truth?"

No. It remained that simple. When my brother rang me last week, I didn't want to deal with him then. Or her. However, it appeared she wasn't going to take 'no' as an answer. Nor would Stan. Until a few days ago, he didn't even have a clue where I'd disappeared to all of those years ago. When we'd reconnected, I'd been rather vague about most of what I'd done and where I'd been.

Some things were best left buried.

Yikes, now he'd discovered so much more than he ever bargained for about his big sister. Well, half-sister. Our lives had crossed for a lightning flash when we both were young. During the early years of our parents' volatile relationship. He'd barely been out of diapers when I'd fled the scene. And that had been more years ago than I cared to remember. We both had grown old and lived a lifetime since. Stan most likely had as many regrets as I did by now.

Or maybe not.

Twisting the phone cord for a moment, I debated again if I should or should not take the bait. Spill out all of my secrets once and for all. Just let the dam burst and flood Stan with everything I've been holding back. But that wouldn't solve anything in the end. All that would accomplish would be creating a deeper divide between us. One that I didn't see a way to build a bridge across. We didn't have that kind of open and honest relationship.

Hell, we didn't have any type of relationship.

"I already gave you all the information you'll ever need." I slammed down the receiver of the old-fashioned landline with a satisfying thunk. Then, I spun on my heel and stomped towards the door. I'd never bothered to sign up for cellphone service, there'd never been anyone to call but Stan. And right at this second, I wondered how great of an idea getting in touch with him had been.

Yanking hard on the old brass knob, the frame groaned as the door popped open. Leaving it wide, I slapped the screen door sending it flying out. All to end up having it hit the wooden log wall of the cabin and bounce back at me, biting at my bare toes as it returned. Elbowing it hard, I shifted as I continued my march onto the porch.

Stopping for an instant or two, I surveyed the trees and grassy fields off to my right. They led down towards a small valley where a small stream fed their thirsty roots. The high mountain desert began at the edge of the raggedly trimmed browning lawn in front of me. Sagebrush, a few cacti, and scraggly weeds led up into the low hills all around.

After a beat or two of my aching heart, my raging emotions began to ebb. I turned to gain a better view of the treeline following the underground aquifer. A mixture of old knotty pine and aspens. My head swiveled around as I tried to take in every last bit of what lay before me. My eyes focusing for the most part on the riot of colors from the autumn leaves.

Deep reds, golds, rusts, mixed with these darker greens, perfect visuals for any artist.

Standing for a slight pause, I breathed in deep the rich aromas. Pine mixed with the dampness left over from last night's storm. Letting my eyelids flutter shut, I allowed the stillness to invade my tormented soul. My heart debated for a second about turning around and putting brush to canvas. Work out my issues as I always did, in dark hues and wide slashes.

But I didn't wish to revert to my old ways, my old work.

Peeling open my eyes, I focused on the brightness, the wonder around me. Allowing it to shift the raging storm inside me. My anger having abated, I slinked over to the worn porch swing and sank into its waiting pillows. Wrapping myself in the blanket I always kept there, I chewed on my lower lip as I pondered the best thing to do. I had no right to be so enraged to have her find me, to want to connect with me. She'd done nothing wrong. Jenny. Her name was Jenny. Or at least that's what Stan had said last week.

My fury and frustration at this situation had been with myself not her.

Tears washed down my cheeks, the view became lost in a watery wave. I had wished the world for her. Even asked the nuns to send her into it with a tiny token of my love, made with my own two hands. Hard to believe she actually had received it, understood I might remember it. That she might see that little outfit for what it was, a hug from me to this unknown child of mine. All of those years ago, my heart had been broken when I hadn't been allowed to even see her little face.

And it had never healed.

So many things I did after she'd been ripped from me - all to ease the pain, which, in the end, had only made things worse. Road after road I'd traveled and they'd all been wrong. Because you can't run from yourself. Your shadow chases you, haunting you with every little misstep you've ever done. In my case, I'd lived in that darkness for years. Allowing it to consume every part of me.

In the end, this was where my rage lay. At myself, for proving everyone right, I wasn't anything more than a slut who deserved the very bad hand she'd been dealt. And for darn sure I didn't want my child to find out any of this. I had a feeling she hated me enough for what little she might already be aware of, no point adding more fuel to that fire. Why after all of this time did she want to connect? And what more did she wish to learn? Or did she need something?

I couldn't even begin to guess at answers to any of these questions.

However, beneath everything lay so much guilt. I'd allowed the most precious thing I would ever be given to become lost, alone out in the great big world. Who had cared for her when she scraped her knee? Who had dried her tears when her first crush broke her heart? Who had helped her prepare for her wedding? Who had cheered when she graduated from college? Who helped when her children were born?

Were those mythical parents she'd been sent to better than me?

Yes, somehow, deep inside me I sensed this child of mine had become a better woman than I had ever been. She'd done something with her life that had meaning and purpose. She'd moved past her disaster of a birth and done something great. Because she'd been raised in a real home. Filled with love. Filled with hope. Filled with peace. Filled with everything she ever wanted.

Unlike me who'd been raised with nothing.

I held onto that slim thread of hope for the nameless, faceless, genderless child of mine for years. That wherever he or she might be would be the perfect place. I didn't care if those parents had money, a big house or a fancy car. All I wanted for my child was to be raised in a house where no one yelled. Or beat someone for not making the bed. Or everyone had to walk on eggshells because they didn't know what horrible thing would happen next. In short, I wanted the opposite of what my life had been for my child.

"Hey, Miss Donna, ya okay?" A soft voice wafted into my ears, pulling me back to reality, out of my dark thoughts.

Brushing my hand against my eyes, I attempted to focus on my visitor standing at the bottom of the porch steps. Timothy, of course.

His mother sent him by almost every day to check on me. I'd been their only permanent tenant for a few years now. Come to think of it, this might have been the longest I'd ever lived anywhere. For me, this backwoods corner of the universe had become a perfect sanctuary. Far removed from the constant state of turmoil my life had remained in for years.

At the end of a long, windy, dirt road, hidden from everyone, I loved the peace I found in this part of New Mexico. When I'd first discovered the listing on some internet site, I'd planned to stay a few weeks. But the tiny one-bedroom cabin with the gorgeous mountain views soothed my heart. And did so in a way few other places had.

And of course, travel restrictions changed my plans in the end.

By this stage in my life, only Stan remained as my lone string attaching me to the world. No other friends or family left. Fine, with my lifestyle there'd never really been friends. And after what had happened with my stepfather when I was in my teens, no family to speak of either. Deep in me, I remained unsure if I'd done the right thing by reaching out to Stan after so many years. We'd never been close for more than a few reasons. Yet a tiny bit of me pitied him, he'd endured so much more than I. Which I hadn't been aware of until I'd found the courage to call him shortly before landing here.

And even then, he'd been an afterthought.

Turning my gaze towards Timothy, I looked over at him, going from the top of his head to his worn work boots. His slim frame made him appear younger than his nineteen years. His faded blue and white flannel shirt worn as a jacket hung off his shoulders. He'd left it unbuttoned, flapping a smidge in the faint breeze. His cotton t-shirt bore the logo of some band I'd heard in concert once – in the seventies. His jeans tattered but clean. Even with my limited knowledge of how this place worked, I'd been able to observe how few visitors showed up. Yes, there were some ten odd cabins in the small compound they ran. But mine tended to be the only one with a guest in it most nights. I could sit on my porch and forget the world because no other lights could be seen but mine.

Money had to be tight for this family.

"I'm not sure, Tim." I noticed he shifted to stand a mite straighter at this, most likely I was the only one to talk to him like he was a man. "It's been one of those mornings."

"Anything I can help with?" He shifted his weight from one foot to the other. He cocked his head, then grasped the railing and began to climb the steps.

I wanted to call out, 'Stop!' Because this space had become mine by default after all this time. I didn't want anyone to invade it. Which is why I insisted that Carol, his mother, allow me to clean my rental, over her vehement objections. This young man had been told my feelings on the matter as well. But something tugged at my heart, something about me had to be off for Timothy to break my unwritten rule.

No, not something, everything.

Never once in all of the time I'd been here had anyone found me sobbing. Not out in public for all the world to see at least. Yes, there'd been those private moments in the dead of night where my pillow ended up soaked. Because I, yet again, drowned myself in a sea of tears. When I would wake up the next morning, my eyes crusted with salt, my face wrinkled and smudged from lack of sleep. That happy-go-lucky hippy I'd been before my pregnancy? She hadn't fully reemerged to see the light of day afterward.

And that was over fifty years ago.

"Sit." I pointed to the plain wooden Adirondack chair in the corner. Its former golden hue long faded into a steel gray as the boards had weathered and aged. The chair and I had so much in common. "Do you have a girlfriend? Any plans beyond this patch of dry grass?"

He eyed me with curiosity as he lowered himself, "Mom don't like me discussing things like that. Well, not since Dad died when I was about twelve at least."

I pushed the floor with my foot setting the swing into motion. "By the time I was your age, I had a child." My voice soft and low. These words I doubt I'd ever spoken out loud before, not sure why exactly I said them now. That whole time in my life locked away, a secret buried deep. Once I'd left the home for unwed mothers, I'd never quite regained my sense of self. Never fully allowed my heart to love again, or even be open to the possibility. Because my very soul had been left in that place.

His eyes widened, then he frowned as he nodded and shook a finger my way. "And the child is now gone, which is why you're crying?"

That was one way to put it. Why do so many people refuse to say the words 'die' or 'death?' They skirt around it and use euphemisms or cliches instead. Not like it's not going to happen to all of us at some point or another. So let's cut out the BS and call it what it is.

However, behind Timothy's simple statement lay so many other layers and truths I didn't want to face. Because in a way, my child had died. Or at least been removed from my life in such a way that I had grieved the loss. Not sure too many others would agree with me on that though.

"No. I gave her up for adoption. But not a day goes by that I don't think about her." I ran my fingers through my long white hair, unsure if I should say more. "Somehow, she found my half-brother, which led her to me. She wants to meet me. Or at least talk to me." I cringed, realizing I hadn't paid much attention to Stan when he'd called.

My thoughts from earlier were spot on, I didn't have the faintest idea what this child of mine wanted.

He rested his head on the back of the chair, looking up at the porch beams. He placed his hands on his stomach, tapping a finger on the back of one. Silent for a few seconds, his chest rose and fell as he took a few deep breaths. "In all the time you've been here, you've never mentioned having anyone at all. No family, no friends, nothing. Almost like you dropped from outer space. For years you've been our guest, but you've kept us at arm's length. No contact except what we initiate. Yet, now, in the space of a few sentences, I find out you've got a brother and a kid. I've always known you were weird, I mean you dress like a hippy and never leave. But this is some deep-level crazy. No offense."

He had a point, okay, more than one. Since I'd arrived, I hadn't left the property. Not exactly, I did wander into the woods almost every day to take long hikes. However, I didn't go into town. Thus, I relied on them to do my shopping for anything I couldn't order off the internet. I relied on them to mail my artwork when it sold. I relied on them to figure out if I was alive or dead. And at my age, that last one had become rather important.

Because, for reasons I couldn't fully explain, I'd found something here which had caused me to stop. I no longer had the chronic urge to roam. To see so much of the world, to search every nook and cranny. Searching for things I couldn't identify much less obtain. Thus, I had continued to find myself empty and hollow. Well, I think the conversation before I arrived back in America had changed my trajectory in life. Much more so than where I'd landed. That had also been the subtle shift to enable me to reach out to Stan.

Even if he hadn't been the one I'd been seeking.

"None taken. I've been keenly aware for most of my life that I'm more than a few bricks short of a full load. And I'm well aware I will never fit into polite society." Giving a slight chuckle, I tried to picture myself anywhere 'normal' or acting 'normal.' But what was 'normal' anyway? Who defined what could and should be acceptable to others?

I can tell you exactly who - all of those 'nice' and 'polite' people who'd been judging me for years.

"Ah, you fit in here just fine." His face lit up with warmth and something akin to love.

I let that slide, since I hadn't let anything slip about who I was in all the time I'd been their guest. No, I didn't think Carol would refuse to rent to me. Time had changed enough so things like that didn't happen anymore. Or one should hope not at least. But, still, I remained an outlier in the universe, someone who would never belong in any category or role.

"You know what I'm most thankful for, Tim? I'm thankful that the world has changed. No, I take that back, I think everyone has taken things a bit too far. Yet, some things are for the better. Back in the day, it wasn't easy being a single mother. Still isn't I imagine, however, it's a bit more acceptable." I drummed my fingers on the armrest of the swing for a moment, in time with the rhythmic motion of its rocking. I didn't want him to think I believed his mother's life was a walk in the park.

He twisted his lips, his face bunched in thought. "Is that why you gave up your child? You didn't think it would be okay to raise it alone?"

I pondered the question, the easy answer remained the obvious. But so much more lay in my choice all of those years ago. Societal norms were starting to shift but where I ended up had more to do with my lack of options. Trauma inflicted by people who should've helped me, that I never recovered from. Instead I just slapped a band-aid on my broken heart and tried to move on. And I still found it hard to think about everything that had happened in my past because of that.

"Before I explain that, how about I tell you more about how I ended up with a brother?" Those wounds were deep, but not as painful. And as I sat here staring at the desert before me, I could hear the sharpness in Charles's voice. Didn't matter how many years had passed. Some things can't be pushed out no matter how hard you try.

He eagerly nodded yes. Sitting for a spell on my porch had to be better than whatever chores he ought to be doing for his mother.

CHAPTER 2

Upstate New York – 1950's - 1965

I don't believe I was ever told what happened to my father, or if in fact, there was a mention of one. I'm not even sure if my mother knew who my father was. I think I just accepted life being the two of us. There were too many other issues in life to worry about something that wasn't even there.

We never had much, I often would eat supper with the neighbors not because they had kids my age. But because there wasn't a scrap of food in our apartment. They were an older couple, immigrants from somewhere and I didn't understand half of what they said. Not like that mattered, they had plenty to eat and never said 'no' when I knocked on their door.

From my youngest memories, my mother, Sharon, had lots of 'friends', some of them more special than others. Then along came Charles when I was about ten. My mother's new mantra became, 'Everything's going to be better now.' Didn't seem that way to me, we still didn't have anything. Not like I'd ever sass back to my mother.

After a few months of visits from Charles, the other men slowly trickled down to nothing. My mother's focus became set on Charles alone. He started showing up almost every day, with little gifts like chocolates or flowers. Not long after that, she told me I was going to have a real 'Daddy' like other kids. I didn't care one way or the other.

We began to pack up our few belongings in our tiny one-bedroom apartment. A place where I always slept in the living room on the lumpy, smelly, beat up, old brown couch. We didn't own the furniture, or even the pots and pans for pity sake. Thus, a few boxes of my things were pretty much all we took with us down the three flights of stairs. The building was a nondescript brick row home, sandwiched in the middle of the block. Nothing special about it or us. My mother had bought a new dress for the occasion, a little white number showing off her cleavage a little too much. But flowing over her stomach just enough to hide the bump that now had become rather obvious.

"Honey, allow me." Charles gushed as he helped her into the car, and didn't notice me at all.

Leaving me to struggle into the backseat with our stuff, thanks a lot.

Our first stop on that day, the courthouse. No fancy wedding for these two. I remained perched on a small chair in an outer office, off the main entrance. My mother had decreed I stay put. The place where the official ceremony would be was far too little for the three of us to enter. My head swiveled back and forth as I watched the odd assortment of people parading before me. Trying to decide if any of them might be better to go home with than my mother and Charles.

After what for me was an eternity, my mother emerged from the depths of the halls. Charles wrapped around her arm, all smiles. "Ready, Donna?" She asked me, like I'd been dawdling of my own choice for hours.

I nodded, dragging my feet a bit as I followed the two lovebirds back to the car.

At Charles's house, I had a bedroom all to myself in the rambling four bedroom place in suburbia. My mother had achieved *the* dream. White picket fence surrounding a manicured lawn. Pink and white rose bushes lining the drive. White mansion with black shutters set high up on a hill. All with a man whom she believed would provide for her every

' need, want, wish. But to me, none of it mattered.

My heart longed for our old home and the feeling of safety I had sensed there. With the neighbors who, on the odd occasion, would provide me with a few scraps to fill my belly. Or a kind word to get me through the day.

At first, Charles appeared sweet and generous to us. My mother's belly began to swell with the child who would be my new baby brother or sister. Yet, the closer to the due date she got, the more he made little comments. He'd slip in words about me, about not being part of 'his' family or just being along for the ride. It was clear to me he saw me as an added unwanted burden.

Then came that fateful moment when I'd been left alone with him for several days. My mother had been whisked away to the hospital, where she would give birth to Stan, leaving me to fend for myself. I'd burnt Charles's dinner, what did I know about cooking? I was eleven at the time. That was the first time he backhanded me, and it soon became a daily habit of his.

And things only went downhill from there. The baby cried? Well, Charles would go into a rage and either break things or hit my mother. I didn't clean the house properly? Yup, I got the tarnation beat out of me. Years and years went by, and his bouts of anger grew worse. And the amount of alcohol involved also steadily increased. Both Charles and Sharon soon started the day with breakfast mimosas. And they ended the evening with whisky sours.

Tempers and glasses would always fly by the end of the night.

There were days my mother couldn't go out of the house. She'd be so battered and bruised, and not wanting others to comment. Days where my mother called my school claiming I'd gotten 'sick' but in fact, the marks on my face were a bit too obvious. We suffered, silent, both pretending it wasn't what it was.

Why my mother allowed this to go on, I didn't have a clue. But by the time I was fifteen, I'd had enough and I decided to fight back.

I fixed dinner, as usual, after I came home from school that late winter day. I hadn't quite finished my homework. Which, by the way, I never did get around to completing most nights. Which resulted in me turning in many blank pages or partial assignments. And my grades were evident of this - C's or D's for the most part.

On this particular night, Mother, Stan, and Charles sat around the dining room table. Mother had laid the table with a pretty pink and white checked tablecloth. The good silverware shone in the twinkling light. A long white tapered candle set in a silver candlestick in the middle. Everything the way Charles liked it. Because everything always had to be the way he preferred it, or else. The dishes were the best of those left unbroken in the house, my mother unable to keep up with the destruction. She did try, about once a month she went to the thrift store and bought replacements.

And same as always, Charles found something he disliked about the meal.

"Donna, the peas are slimy, you put too much butter on them again. I'm not made of money, you know butter's expensive. Don't waste it by making the food taste bad! And the rolls aren't hot, make sure you heat them properly so they aren't hard. I hate them that way!" He started to rise from his chair, raising his arm.

Stan cowered in his chair, sliding towards the floor as he had a habit of hiding under the table for things like this. At not quite four, all he'd witnessed in his short life had been the evil side of his father. Not that he'd ever experienced the pain of a punch or a slap. No, he'd only been an innocent bystander, watching helplessly what had been done to my mother and I.

My mother bowed her head, holding the table so hard her knuckles went white. She never stepped in to stop Charles, no, she'd just looked away. Well aware that she might be next even if she remained quiet.

Tonight, my body vibrated with rage. Every inch of me ready to face down this man who'd been terrorizing me for years.

Quick as lightning, I hopped up, my chair flying backward as I did so. I swung a punch, landing it squarely on Charles's nose, much to my surprise. The bright red spots dribbling out were both shocking and delightful to my eyes. I'd won, for about half a second.

He put a hand up to his face to stop the flow, "Get the hell out of my house! You and your whore of a mother!"

Without blinking, I gazed deep into his eyes and saw them narrow and darken. The veins on his forehead and neck pulsed. I'd seen this before and ended up with so many bruises I couldn't go to school the next day. Deep inside me, I said '*No, never again!*'

I wanted to yell in defense of my mother. I also wanted to take another swing or two at this man. I understood what would happen if I continued to engage with this angry man. All I would achieve would be to provoke him further. Thus, with my head held high, I stalked out of the room. Marched right down the front hall, out the door, into the street.

And never looked back.

Not my best move, but the only one I could come up with in the heat of the moment. I had nothing but my pride and anger to keep me going. I stomped around for a few hours, not caring about the chill of the evening. Not worrying about the fact I didn't have a jacket and there was still a light layer of snow on the ground. My anger kept me warm.

I ended up finding myself in front of my best friend Julia's door. My feet had led me there without my brain giving it any thought at all. Standing there, I had a raging debate in my head about knocking or not. After all, wouldn't her parents just call mine? And if they did, Charles would kill me if I dared to show my face in his home again. And I did believe in the full meaning of that word.

In the end, I weaved my way around the dormant rose bushes. Their bare branches reaching out to catch at my pants as I hugged them to stay out of the light. Onward I went to the backyard and Julia's window. The house, dark and foreboding, everyone in bed for the night, much too late to come calling. Giving a timid tap on the glass, I gave out a loud sigh as I looked over my shoulder to the garden shed. Wondering if it was locked or not.

A creak from behind me caused me to snap my head back toward the house. A white shape fluttered into view as the curtains slid open a mite, causing my heart to stop and my whole body to tense. As the sash rose an inch more, a voice drifted out into the night, "Whatever are you doing silly?"

I almost wet myself before I realized it was Julia. But why hadn't she turned on a light? "Help me up and I'll explain." I reached out a hand to push up the window wider as I began to wiggle myself into the open space.

She huffed but complied. A moment later I tumbled onto the floor, a giggling heap from the effort to haul myself into the house. She closed the window, then slid onto the floor next to me, wrapping us both with a warm blanket she pulled from her bed.

"Spill." She nudged me hard with an elbow. Julia and I had become fast friends. On that first day I'd started at my new school after Mother and I'd moved in with Charles. We'd been inseparable ever since and she was the only one I'd allowed to see a few of my bruises over the years. I'm sure this is why, in my hour of desperation, I'd ended up here without even thinking about it.

"I'm done. I don't care where I'm going, but I'm leaving town." Squeezing my eyes tight, I tried to picture what kind of future I wanted. All I saw were stars and an empty void. When your life is nothing but terror after terror, it's impossible to think beyond the next second. You don't plan for next week, next year, next anything. Because you're very aware that you probably won't be given that time. This second is all you have, no more. My grades at school barely passable, no outside interests, nothing.

And I told her everything, all that I'd held back about what had been happening behind closed doors. What my mother had been like before, what she was like now, and who Charles had turned out to be.

She wrapped me in her arms, sobbing like I'd told her I had two days to live until we both succumbed to our emotional exhaustion and drifted off to sleep.

My eyelashes wouldn't budge, like they were glued together. I rubbed them gently with my fingers to remove the gunk. As I slowly opened them, I noticed the first few rays of pink. Dawn crept into the still-open curtain above us, shadows shifted. Julia and I were entwined in a heap on the large floor pillows. I needed a plan, not to wallow in self-pity like I had the night before. Pushing myself into a seated position, I gazed at my friend.

Was her perfect life really that perfect?

She shifted, rubbing her eyes before opening them as well. "Hey there." She remained snuggled in the blanket, staring at me. "Feeling better?"

How to answer that? It wasn't as if I had a cold or something. This wasn't something that would go away with time. Charles deep down contained the essence of some malevolent being. No ounce of kindness remained within him. It'd been a false front he'd shown my mother before their wedding. Nodding, I struggled to stand. "Guess I'll be heading out now before your parents figure out I'm here."

She gnawed on a knuckle, deep in thought for a second. She twisted her lip, squinted one eye. Then jumped up and ran to her closet, her long white nightgown flying behind her. Kneeling, she crawled deep into the recesses pushing things aside as she did. "Yes!" Echoed back into the room as she wiggled her way out. Plopping onto her backside, she held a steel coffee can in her hands.

"Donna, I want you to have this." She tapped on the lid of the can, huffing and panting as she did. "This is all of my Christmas, birthday, chore, and well, you get the idea, all of my money." She gave me a wicked little grin, "My daddy thinks I'm his princess and I make him pay for everything. I've never touched this at all!"

My eyelashes fluttered as I tried in vain not to cry, I swallowed the rock in my throat before I squeaked out a reply. "Oh, sweety, I can't. It's too much..."

She rose, taking a few steps towards me. Taking my hands in hers, she wrapped mine around the can. "Nonsense. You need it and I never will." She rocked back on her heels, moving an inch or so from me. She tapped on her chin as she raised her head. "You know my brother's friend, Tony?"

I nodded; words were beyond me at this point.

"His cousin, hum, I don't remember his name, oh never mind, not important. Anyway, this cousin has a house a couple of towns from here and lets just about anyone flop there." She pointed out the window with her hand, half waving towards some distant point.

And I said goodbye to my friend a few minutes later. One of her purses slung on my shoulder filled with her money. Her suitcase clutched in my hand with a few items of her clothes in it. A note tucked in my pocket with Tony's phone number. But most importantly, I had a plan. One that included me not saying my real age. Nope, now I was sixteen – I'd aged a whole year in one night. Because at sixteen I believed people wouldn't consider me a kid anymore. Which they would if they thought I was fifteen. I wanted to be seen and judged as an adult. To stand on my own.

Silly of me to be worried about something so trivial as my age, I'm well aware. I had much bigger problems facing me.

CHAPTER 3

New Mexico – Present Day

"Wait, what? You ran away from home as a kid?" Timothy leaned forward, elbows on his knees, hands held up with palms open, eyes wide. "As in, legit, never went home again?"

I nodded, unsure what to say in response. In a way, that had been my best decision at the time, and I think it might have saved me from a worse fate. But in so many others it remained the worst thing I'd ever done. So often I pondered those 'what ifs' and how many things could have been different if I'd gone home that day. However, in the end, even if I had stayed, I don't see how I could've changed the outcome. Not for my mother, not for Stan, not for me. Yet deep in the back of my mind I wanted to scream so many things to my younger self. Traps to avoid, places to not go, shame to not heap upon my head.

Men to not have gone anywhere with.

"When exactly was this? Sometime in the seventies? No offense, but I'm not sure how old you are." He gave me a sheepish grin. "But wasn't it kinda okay to just take off back then? I mean, what with all those communes and things."

Ah, the innocence of youth and difference of perspectives of another generation. "Thanks for the confidence boost, Tim. However,

I'm talking nineteen sixties. I'm a bit older than I look, I guess. And I don't think there ever was a moment in history where it was fine with anyone for a fifteen-year-old girl to take off. Or to end up shacked up with a bunch of college age men." I shook my head, more in frustration at myself than at his reaction.

What he didn't know was the attitude my mother modeled. That my body was my biggest and only asset from my earliest memory. And I ended up using this knowledge I'd learned from her to my full advantage. Or so I'd allowed myself to believe for a long time.

But sex wasn't to be thrown around so casually.

Until I met Bruce, I'd flirt, tease, and sleep with anyone to obtain what I wanted and needed. No matter how disgusted about myself this made me feel inside. I stuffed down the icky sensations in my stomach, the dread crawling up my spine. Plaster on a fake smile warm enough to melt an iceberg bigger than Mt. Everest. And never let on I wasn't having a grand time.

I grew up fast, becoming a woman who could read a room in an instant and figure out which man to prey on in the blink of an eye. Others viewed me as sexy and coy, not seeing what lay beneath was a scared child who just wanted to be loved.

And not in the way a man loves a woman.

But with Bruce everything changed. Our love became so intense we sensed each other's deepest hurts and needs without anything being said. That kind of love held power. And if the magic lasts, there's no wrong that can't be undone within such a bond. However, I'd learned through the years, humans are incapable of producing that kind of love for the most part. And Bruce and I were fated from the start to be unable to keep our love growing and strong.

Timothy grimaced for a moment, as he tucked and crossed his arms across his chest. I'm sure all manner of unpleasant images were flashing through his mind. "But you did call your mother at some point, right? I mean, she was your mom, she deserved to find out where you landed."

He hesitated for a beat, wrinkling his nose. "And if you were okay."

"Not for years, and by then it was too late for both of us." I bit my lower lip as I tapped on it with a fingernail. I knew full well, if that brief conversation had gone the way I'd hoped, I wouldn't be sitting here at this moment. However, I went too far for even my mother to be willing to save me. "And there was so much that happened in between."

He stroked his chin, the hint of stubble that lay there he picked at for a moment. "Don't think most kids are totally honest with their mothers. There's a conversation I need to have with mine, but I don't know how to start it or even what to say. I'm sure she's going to be hurt if I do bring the subject up." He shook his head, a wave of doubt washing over his whole countenance.

I wasn't anyone's Mother, well, not in the full meaning of that word. Thus, it wasn't my place to say anything here. But at the look of pain and worry on his face, it would be odd if I didn't respond at all. I should at least give a platitude or two. But those types of words lay outside my field of expertise so to speak. I had tried my best for so long to stay away from the difficulties of others.

"Your mom seems like a very caring and sympathetic person. Whatever it is you need to work out, it's my gut feeling, she'd listen to you and be able to understand where you're coming from. My mother had a bunch of problems in her life that your mother doesn't. You shouldn't think our situations are even a tiny bit similar." I tried to shoot him a small smile, and failed.

"But what if it's something she did, not something I did?" He grimaced as he shifted his gaze from me to the stained floor boards. Tapping his foot, he pressed his palm into his knee to still this anxious tick.

Gulping hard, I pulled on a seam of my patchwork skirt. Switched to tracing a finger around one of the many flowers in the various patterns sewn into it. I guess both of us needed this chat today. Which explains why he had bucked up and been bold enough to march up my steps. Doubt he'd given more than a passing thought to my distress. It wasn't anything more than an opening to have someone to share his burden with. However, he didn't know me, didn't understand how much of a hot mess I had always been.

Didn't comprehend that I should be the last person to turn to for any kind of help.

"Have you tried to talk to anyone else about this? Teacher, priest, pastor, friend?" Yup, this was one buck I needed to pass.

He shook his head 'no' before giving me a sideways glance. "But what she did, well, what she and my father did to be accurate here, affects me. I kinda would like some answers."

I tugged on the tassel tie of my white peasant top, trying to think of something helpful to suggest. Giving a slight shrug, I curled my lips inward and decided to ignore his issues for now. "Well, for me, finding answers usually led to more problems. Maybe it's best to just let it be."

"Okay." A look of disappointment washed over his face, he'd expected so much more from me. "So where'd ya go when you ran away?"

"All over the place." My shoulders dropped a bit as the tension in me lowered. I don't allow myself to become close to people, to share in some kind of common experience. Their burdens are as heavy as mine, as complex as mine. I didn't like being put on the spot, like the one Timothy had just put me in.

Don't ask me to solve whatever is wrong in your life, whatever issues you have, I have enough of my own to deal with.

CHAPTER 4

Upstate New York, Texas – 1965 - 1967

As I left Julia's house that morning, I marched down the street with my head held high. Determined to have everything come up roses from now on. In my young mind, life seemed so simple to me. I didn't have to do anything I didn't want to do. No one had the right to treat me the way Charles had.

My fate, I alone could decide.

After I found an all-night diner, I sat there for a few hours. Swirling overly sweetened and whitened coffee with my spoon, not taking a sip. My feet propped on my suitcase, trying to hide it from prying eyes. Staring at the shiny gold flakes in the pink Formica tabletop, ignoring the world. As I waited for it to be a more decent hour than just after five a.m. to call Tony.

When I popped the coin in the payphone, my stomach dropped into my shoes. *Why is he going to help you?* You're *just the friend of his friend's kid sister!* Gripping the receiver with all my might, I waited for someone to answer the many rings. My heart beating heavy, hurting like it had turned to stone in my chest. My hand shaking, sweating, as I tried not to cry out in despair.

"Hello?" Deep, husky, breathless.

I explained who I was and why I was calling, and got a, "Sure, no worries." response. Ten minutes later, Tony arrived at the diner in his beat-up royal blue Packard, more rust than anything. He didn't move an inch from his position in the driver's seat to help me. Leaving me to haul my large, heavy suitcase into the backseat myself. As I slid into the front, I adjusted my red wool plaid skirt and put my hands in my lap as I did.

"Thanks for this," I murmured, prim and proper as could be.

He gave no reply as we drove in silence through the early morning streets. As we pulled out of town, he slipped his hand onto my thigh, tapping his fingers against my leg as he did. I brushed it off like any other annoying insect and adjusted myself to be closer to the cold door. I'd seen men do this to my mother, and what she did in response.

Not for me.

"So that's how you're going to play this?" He asked, tilting his head a bit so he could give me a quick glance.

"I'll give you money for gas." My voice flat and even, every inch of me growing colder by the second.

"Fine." He snorted, "But I doubt that Sammy is going to be that easy."

And it hit me, this is why my mother had all of those 'friends' before Charles, and why she didn't have a job. I'd seen all of the ogling stares men would give her when they'd show up at our apartment at all hours of day and night. She never wore anything but her lacy white nightgown and matching lacy white robe. I don't think she had ever owned but the one dress before we'd moved in with Charles. An overly tight green dress that her chest almost popped out of and showed her knees and half of her thighs. And that dress she only wore the few times she went to buy groceries. But always managed to come home with almost no food. Nope, she'd have a guy on her arm instead. All of these guys would show up at our place and would put their hands all over her. Yet she never seemed to mind, often she'd move it to a more intimate place. Then she'd tell me to not make any noise and take them to her bedroom. Where the two of them would make lots of noise. Even the landlord came, at least once a month, and was escorted to her bedroom.

Those men were her job.

Until something had gone wrong and she'd gotten pregnant with Stan. Which is how we'd ended up living with Charles, his temper and his beatings. Was Charles even the right guy? Or had my mother picked him because he appeared to be the safest bet? The guy with the most money? Didn't matter now why he'd been the one. I wasn't going to follow in my mother's footsteps. There had to be another way.

But for almost two years, I found out, there really wasn't.

I had no skills in much of anything, and boy did I regret I hadn't paid much attention to my lessons in school. All of those typing sessions, dictation instructions, and so much more. Skills I should've learned to find a job as a secretary or something with some dignity. But, no, I'd played around and hadn't done much of anything in my classes. Technically, I'd ignored everything to take care of Charles and the house to avoid getting beaten to a pulp. But who's counting?

Either way, never doing my homework had left me unprepared for life.

Unfortunately, wrapping men around my little finger was as natural to me as breathing. At Sammy's house, I became queen bee in no time flat. Of the ten or so people that flopped there, I could make most of them do my bidding no problem at all. The other girls viewed me with more than a touch of suspicion. They didn't want me to gain too much influence on the boys they had already staked a claim on. Yet, I only needed to keep one person in this situation satisfied, the one who controlled the house – Sammy.

But Sammy turned out to be too handsy, and in a few months I needed to move on. I didn't like to be groped from morning till night just to keep a roof over my head and a few scraps in my belly. Didn't feel the need to say I might be leaving or nothing. Just walked out one day with everything I owned and a few things I didn't.

I didn't want to turn into my mother.

I'd heard of a group heading out west, maybe California, and I'd asked if I could join. At the time they seemed harmless enough. Their old school bus overflowed with unkempt bodies. Plus the scent of weed, music from someone's guitar. The bus was painted inside and out in a shade of bright pink. Big flowers in a variety of colors, peace signs and white birds wove around the sides. Everyone seemed so laid back, casual, escaping the world. No rules, no wrongs, no rights, do what feels good.

Peace, love, and happiness.

As I wandered, I learned what was important for survival in this new life of mine. Avoiding the guys who would push too far. How to use the rhythm method to avoid getting in the family way. And to never stay in the same place for very long. Somewhere along the way, I traded my clunky suitcase for a backpack. As I began to peel off what had been me, I discovered there wasn't much underneath.

New clothes, new attitude, new life far from home. All surrounding the empty shell of the person that I would always be.

I swapped the group in the bus for a group in a different bus or WV van, or whatever, over and over again. It didn't matter who I hung out with, as long as I remained a rolling stone or a bit of dandelion fluff floating in the wind. Unattached, unemotional, unfeeling, uncaring.

Sure I tried to go with the flow and look like a flower child on the outside. But something didn't sit well with me about the whole thing. I needed more, a vague thing that remained just beyond my reach no matter how far I roamed. And boy did I wander over those few years. Concerts, protest marches, communes, mountains, beaches, cities.

Yet nothing felt safe, comfortable, good.

How I ended up in West Texas, I'm not entirely sure. One day in late spring after about two years of being on the road, I hopped out of some van I'd been in for far too long. Took a good look around the town

I found myself in. Determined to do something, anything else.

This little bump on the road had a tiny college, great for me, so many choices of young men to stay with. I'd hang out on campus and have my pick of those I'd spotted lounging on the quad. By fall, I'd run through almost everyone. Every inch of me had become anxious and antsy, ready to move on, find something new.

However, something happened, something I never expected, or wanted. I gave my heart away.

I hated the party scenes. However, for my purposes they worked well and were lucrative hunting grounds. When everyone else was stoned or drunk or both, manipulation came easy without very high of a cost on my part. I'd pretend to partake the booze and drugs with everyone else but never did. Thus, my plan for that major back to school bash had been to walk away with as much cash as possible. Without having to do anything to earn it. Then I'd be able to leave town without any worries and float for a while.

Yes, by seventeen, I'd learned many skills and most of them I shouldn't have.

I entered the crowded room, scanning as I always did for those boys I'd already had used and tossed aside. Didn't want to have a scene with them being upset at me for my wanton behavior. I made my way around the space packed with gyrating bodies. As I did so, I made sure to give attention to those boys who I sensed I might still get something out of. A gentle rub on the shoulder here, a peck on the cheek there, a whisper of encouragement maybe. All the while, I picked their pockets clean.

No, I'm not proud of what I did. To my deep shame, I'd become a version of my mother, the one thing I'd never wanted to be.

I loathed every dime I got this way. I longed for the day when I would figure out my life enough to do something, anything else. But there never seemed to be an opportunity. Or, to be more precise, a safe place to put down some roots for more than a hot minute. The face I showed to the world hid the frightened child I remained. Everything scared me, yet I pressed on in life because I didn't believe I had any other options open to me.

No one had ever modeled for me a different way of living.

Out of the corner of my eye, I spotted someone new. And he wasn't a boy like all the others and he didn't belong with this lot. He was mature, strong, stiff. As I continued to make my rounds, I scrutinized him from the corner of my eye. Trying to work out why he'd ended up in this scene, why he didn't stalk out in a huff at the debauchery around him.

This was a man, in every sense, not a college boy here to fool around.

He sat ramrod straight, in the far recesses of the dining room. Dressed in what for all the world appeared to be church attire, black pants and light blue dress shirt. He hugged his beer as if it remained the sole anchor. The one thing keeping him connected to the world outside of the chaos that was this party. So out of his element my heart ached as I sneaked peeks at him.

Yet there remained a simple truth which kept me gazing at him every few seconds. He had something I wanted and needed. Something elusive, something I couldn't quite put my finger on. Yet, I craved whatever he had which enabled him to remain so still and quiet in the madness. After fleecing everyone I could think of for as much as I could, I made my way to the stranger.

I played my game, swaying my hips as I drew near, dancing my fingers on the table. His eyes grew larger and larger, his chest drew in as his breathing stopped. Goodness, the guy might pass out on me before I could do anything more than flirt. *Has he never been with a girl?* I shuddered for a second at the thought. His beer can clattered to the floor, splashing liquid everywhere. And I debated about putting him out of his misery, to turn around, walk away before any harm was done. But something in the look he gave me drew me in, forcing me to stay.

As he started to stand, I pushed him back into the chair. As I sank into his lap, determination to weave my magic spell over him filled every inch of me. But as I began to stroke his short brown hair, every vibe coming off of him continued to be tension and tightness. After what seemed an eternity, his hand moved. He pulled ever so slightly on the large holes in my loose peach-colored crocheted vest. I figured it would be the only form of reciprocation he would ever be able to give. He didn't have a clue what to do with a woman.

"You're the only one here not having fun," I whispered in his ear, "Why?"

He panted hard, his hand dropping back to his side. Pain written all over his face. "Doesn't seem like my kind of scene."

I'd never had this hard of a time getting anyone to succumb to my charms before, he now became a puzzle I needed to solve. I slid my hands into his shirt, undoing the top few buttons as I did so. To try to help him relax, I played with his chest and stomach. Tender massaging touch as I worked my way down, my goal to go all the way to his pants. "Well, what is?"

As I leaned in to give him a little peck on his cheek, he turned his head and answered, "I'm not sure."

Thus, I created a real kiss, pushing hard against him for a moment so that he would taste my tongue on his lips. I moved my head back a fraction to gauge how he handled this much contact from me.

Given his look of surprise at our rather simple smooch, I gingerly slipped my hand out of his shirt. Not completing my task. I'd tortured the guy enough. I patted his cheek before kissing my fingers then pressing them to his lips. Throwing him my best coy smile, I raised my eyebrows towards the back door. As gentle as I could, I took his meaty paw into my slim fingers as I rose from his lap. His arm still stiff as a board, I gave him a slight tug to indicate he should follow me. He, as awkwardly as a newborn lamb, rose to his feet.

Pulling him along, we weaved through the crowd, ignoring the noise. The sliding glass door already had been pushed to its full open point. Allowing us to sail through without slowing. Having been to a party or two at this location, I was aware couples would be out on the grass, thus, I glided past them as well. I wanted privacy for what I planned to do next, I had an ideal spot in mind. After I managed to maneuver us out into the alley, I hoped we were in a quiet enough of a place for some form of intimacy. But the more important point had to be to bring some measure of calm to this man, have him be in less of a panic mode. Resting my head on his shoulder, slipping my arm into his, we began a slow swinging stride toward the park.

But his heart continued to race, his breaths continued to be labored. For whatever reason, releasing his internal pressure valve didn't seem possible. Tempted as I was to run my hands over him, I remained as still as possible. I'd convinced myself I'd only make things worse, he'd end up exploding. I continued to take slow measured lungfuls of the muggy night air. Hoping beyond hope that my peace would cover him. I'd learned yoga and meditation with other hippies over the last few years. But that didn't appear to be doing me any good right at this moment.

As we rounded the corner, I caught a glimpse of his face under the glow of the street lamp. Stern, firm, tight lipped. Not a man out for an evening stroll with a pretty girl wrapped around him.

"Better?" I had to try to break him out of his shell, help him to relax, be comfortable. Not for me, but for him. Something deep inside him held him tight, killing his very soul.

"Maybe. Quiet at least." His eyes stayed focused on the sidewalk in front of us.

"I'm Donna." If he knew my name, he'd come to believe we were friends. That'd help him to loosen up a bit. Right?

"Bruce." Nothing more, just this single word grunted out deep and low.

By then my finish point lay before us, but none of this had gone according to plan. No way to conquer Bruce, he wouldn't be taking me home or anywhere else for that matter. I'd be lucky if I got more than five words out of him and then I would have to stroll back to my current crash pad, alone. Yet, for some reason, right at this moment that was okay.

Leading him to a nearby bench, he stiffly sat down, his whole body ramrod straight. I kicked off my sandals, tucked my feet under my long skirt and leaned against him. We chatted a bit about him and about me. His life on the farm, my leaving home. I sensed that he, like me, hadn't told the whole truth. Or even a truth. I'd merely mentioned something dumb about family drama. Which didn't even scratch the surface of my mother's ill-fated marriage. Or what had taken place afterward.

And I wasn't about to mention what she did before her marriage. Or what I'd done after I'd left home.

And it clicked, what he needed, the missing piece in his life. Fun, laughter, spontaneity. Doing something for himself. Because I also needed those things. Thus, I began to chuckle, light and soft at first, then louder. Bruce joined in, our chortles ringing out into the steamy night air in that tiny Texas town.

We hugged as we laughed and sobbed, releasing those deep down, buried hurts and griefs we didn't want to say. When I believed our catharsis to be over, I swiped the tears from his face, looking deep into his eyes. The deep brown reflected back the gold of the moonlight, his shyness now over. But I didn't wish for him to see the real me. To ever have any clue as to the real reason I'd been at the party. To learn about me being a thief or worse.

Jumping up, I stretched more to distract him than anything while I took a moment to think about my next move. Without stopping to put my shoes back on, I ran to the pond, pulling up short just before the water's edge. Hearing Bruce puffing behind me, I plopped to the ground. His hand stroking my long blonde hair as I curled myself into a tight ball.

Trying to protect him from the harm I could inflict on him, that I might have already done to him.

A single duck floated on the pond, lost and alone in the night.

Staring out beyond the water where there weren't any street lamps, I focused on the darkness. I belonged there, in those shadows where there wasn't light. Because there, one wouldn't be able to witness my deeds, my faults, my flaws, my true nature. My life as I now lived it was best hidden, kept secret. I'd stayed too long here in this place.

I needed to leave now before I damaged Bruce, ruined him and pulled him into something he wasn't ready for. Because with me, everything always leads to, but the one place. Yet, he'd followed me but I decided to give him an out. Send him home, back to some place good where there was nothing but light.

"Do you think I should be like the duck?" I reached up and grabbed his hand, tugging on it hard.

His body thumped to the ground beside me, "What do you mean?"

Ugh, he didn't understand, I'd have to spell it out. "Go home in the spring." I hadn't wanted to look at him, this needed to be up to him alone. Thus, I frowned, not wanting to give him any idea that I wished for anything. Not like I had a home to go to, this was more in the metaphorical sense. Did he want me to leave his town and move on?

His hand in mine gave me a gentle squeeze. "I'm not sure yet." He gave out a slight cough. "Ask me again next week."

I took that as a sign, a very good sign. For me, not for him.

CHAPTER 5

New Mexico – Present Day

"That night changed both our lives. And not for the better, I'm afraid." I sighed as I tried to not see that night in shadow and sorrow. That night needed to remain what it was, innocent and sweet. Untainted by what would come later, for me or for Bruce.

I had so many regrets in life, Bruce had always remained at the top of the list. I could still see him, standing there in the moonlight. Perfect, whole, untouched. I should've left after that night, allowed him to find his own way in life. However, at that point I didn't know much about him beyond the fact he lived on a farm with his mother and he wasn't a party boy.

Would I have made a different choice if I had been aware of his hopes and dreams that first night? As I grew to know and love Bruce, I learned he had this idea to become a veterinarian. He wanted to help farmers with their animals, work for himself, build his own world. He struggled with his classes, science didn't come natural for him. But his determination would've kept that fire lit, kept him fighting for everything he wanted in life.

Until I stepped into the picture.

I used to shove those heavy books out of his hands, tease him, take his focus off the prize he strove for. Why had I ever thought I might be something worth more than what he'd already determined in his heart was best for him? He'd been too ashamed of me to ever introduce me to his mother. All these thoughts tumbled around in my head. And I could see, even now with so much time gone by, that he always saw me as nothing more than a trollop. A quick college fling, his first girl to be tossed aside as soon as the first tiny bump happened.

And a pregnancy wasn't exactly something minor.

Yet, was that being fair to him? Or was I projecting my guilt, my shame onto him? Afterall, going all the way had been my idea. Not his. I'd been told I could handle everything on my own. Because this is what I did. With everything. Was it possible that he viewed me in a very different light than I could ever see myself in?

Shaking my head, I tried to get those ideas out.

Timothy tilted his head, deep in thought. "I'm guessing that Bruce is the father, right?"

I nodded, looking down at the worn porch floor. Appreciating yet again the patterns made by the sun over the years. Patches of darker and lighter hues where the sunlight had been stronger or weaker. Partially blocked by various things like the porch railing or the nearby trees. All ending up shifting over time. The resulting bleaching of the wood at different rates so delicate and intricate. So much more interesting than slapping some stain on it and calling it a day.

Just as scars caused by life can make people more fascinating.

Scrunching up my lips, I opened and closed my hands in my lap. Wishing for nothing more than to apologize to Bruce. For everything from those few months in Texas. For leaving without a trace. I'd taken so much more than I'd given him. I'd left him with a wound so deep that I had no way of knowing if he had ever recovered from it.

How does one forget a child? Or is it different for men? After all, he didn't have an opportunity to put his hand on my stomach as our child kicked inside my womb as I had. Nor did he have moments where he might have been able to whisper little things to this unborn child as I did. I'd left before he could even have had the chance.

Maybe he'd never given us a second thought. Or maybe he'd grieved every day like I had.

"Miss Donna, how much does he know?" Timothy began to tap out a rhythm with his foot, then he coughed slightly. "I'm just asking because I've got a buddy who was adopted. Now that he's over eighteen he's trying to find his birth parents and, trust me, it isn't easy. And he's been told it's way better to find info now than back in the day." The words came out in a rush, poured out from a place of hurt and grief.

Somehow what Timothy had shared didn't quite have the ring of truth to it. However, I couldn't quite figure out what might be wrong with the statement. Was I reading something into this because of my own grief? Or did he have genuine concern for his friend? At the moment, I decided to leave the declaration unanswered and kept the focus on my situation.

"I haven't a clue how much information Bruce may or may not have about our child. My best guess is nothing or everything. That all depends on if Jenny found him as well." Which, of course, can be blamed on me. I ran away after I learned of my pregnancy and then had that horrible fight with Bruce. Had he also left the scene as he said he would? Thus, had we both fled?

Ugh.

Sighing, I focused on a meadowlark who had now perched on the wide railing beside me. He bobbed for a moment, looking at me before giving me a few whistled notes. The bird dipped his head at me before flying off, floating on the wind towards the aspen trees. The bird had done what I always used to do, leave before I finished my song. I hadn't wanted the responsibility that came with life, to be tied to anything, to be trapped. Yet, in the end, I'd ended up losing the most precious thing I'd ever been given.

At the time of our child's birth, I'd laid the blame for giving him or her away squarely on Bruce. He'd forced my hand, I'd been left with no other options. Single, broke, homeless, friendless, no family, nothing but my pride to fuel my anger at the world. I'd tried to survive on my own and failed, falling into a hole with no way out.

This child of mine deserved more, as so many people kept reminding me at the time.

However, we each had a role to play in the drama that led up to the act of creating a baby and culminating in me giving birth. And my deception lay at the core of it all, my actions before my pregnancy resulted in the whole mess afterwards. Not with Bruce alone. But with me being unable to care for an infant. With me ending up with an abusive man afterward. With me never settling down and having a 'normal' life.

I've come to own that now.

Timothy's eyes were glued on me, I had the key to unlocking something he needed. What did I have that he could want so desperately? "You at least told him, right? You didn't just leave him without telling him you were expecting." His hand fluttered before his face for a moment, before landing below his chin. He was struggling with something, unsure if he'd said too much or not enough.

"As I'm sure you've already guessed, Bruce and I didn't have the happily ever after fairy tale romance. In the end, I think I might have destroyed him in more ways than one. Over the years, I've considered trying to find him. However, as I considered everything, I always believed I'd do more harm than good if I tried." I grimaced, there wasn't any easy way to explain away all of the pain I caused, the wounds I'd inflicted.

Not back then, not now, not ever.

He frowned at this non-answer answer. "He did know you were pregnant, right?" I guess he figured I hadn't understood him the first time.

"That's a whole complicated mess." I wasn't about to launch into details of my one weekend with Bruce, but certain truths shouldn't be hidden.

"Isn't life a mess by default?" He ran his fingers through his shaggy dark brown hair, "I didn't have a clue about the whole adoption thing until I was going through a few boxes in the attic."

He'd slipped, and let out something he undoubtedly didn't want to fill me in on quite yet. The conversation he didn't want to have with his mother but still was desperate to have anyway. The thing his parents did. The 'friend' trying to find his birth parents. All of the pieces fit into a rather complex puzzle. How long had he been trying to hold onto this secret? And what had changed to make him this compelled to unburden himself right at this moment?

All the answers I didn't have.

"I'm not sure, Tim. Much of my life has led to one broken bridge after another. Well, who's kidding who? I blew up those bridges. Relationships and I don't mix. To the point that I ended up not following the path of life at all. For the most part, I've been lost in the woods for most of the last thirty years." I grimaced. Such a bad way of describing my life. "Nevermind. But I would hope that most other people have at least some stability in their lives. Take you, for instance, have you always lived here? Not New Mexico, I mean here on this property." I bit my knuckle, not wishing to make this young man's situation any worse. Here's hoping I'd taken the right road for the conversation to go down.

"My parents owned the property before I was born, so always." He laced his fingers, stretched out his arms before putting them behind his head.

I gave a sly grin, "Okay, your parents gave you a great home and raised you right. Doesn't sound like your life was messy in the least." I bit the inside of my cheek, feeling bad about making light of his inner turmoil. "Yeah, I'm sorry your father died when you were so young. But your mom hasn't gone anywhere, she's here and doing her best, yes?"

He gave a bit of a head nod, not willing to acknowledge my point might be spot on. "For the most part."

For reasons I couldn't quite explain, my heart ached for him. He had the Mom I'd always wanted, yet still somehow ended up feeling as lost as I had been at that age. "You found something, didn't you? About your adoption? Or your birth parents?"

He remained completely still. His head resting on the back of the chair, eyelids closed, as his arms began a slow crawl down to his sides. "After I found the papers, I reached out to the adoption agency listed on them, ya know, to find out what the heck was going on. They emailed me last night, my adoption was supposed to be what they call open. But afterward, my parents changed their minds and refused to stay in contact with my birth Mother. The agency believes they know where she is and can contact her for me if that's what I want."

Every inch of me wanted to scream, *'What does this woman who gave birth to you want?! Would she prefer to stay in the shadows? Would she prefer to not have that wound reopened?'* However, my story isn't everyone's. Rules changed, society changed, everything changed in fifty something years. I could say with some confidence that no one had told this woman her pregnancy had landed her in 'trouble.' Made her unlovable, unwanted, unable to do anything right.

"That conversation you don't wish to have but need to have..." I started, hesitating, twirling a strand of my long gray hair around my finger. My own bias about this would color my responses. These had the potential for destroying Tim's chances at ever finding the answers he sought.

He sucked in his lips, his face turning a bit white as anguish filled his eyes. "I've waited too long." He murmured, his eyes fluttering open. "I should've manned up and told her when I first found the paperwork." The words a bit bolder, stronger as he made a fist then thumped his chest. "Now, I've taken things so much farther. And found out that she didn't want me to ever find out about my birth mother."

"But at first, when all you had was a few pieces of paper, did you really have anything to share? Be honest now, had you learned anything useful? Or had you just learned the truth of your birth?" My tone soft, trying to soothe his pain in the one way I thought might bring some comfort.

His fingers began to uncurl, he wiggled them around for a moment as he contemplated my questions. "What did you tell your mother? When you called her? Did you tell her you were pregnant? Or did you call her before that, to tell her about your boyfriend?"

Fine, duck my inquiries. Take a few minutes to distract yourself with anything other than what you're dealing with. Not like I hadn't done that a million times. "I don't think I ever told anyone about Bruce. He was mine and mine alone. Well, for a few months at least. I called my mother after the fact, the way you're thinking you're doing with your problem."

CHAPTER 6

Texas – 1967 - 1968

Over the next several months that fall, I spent as much time on campus as possible. Not because I had made the decision to become a student or even to be a bit more responsible. No, my aim became stalking Bruce. My sole purpose in life became finding a way to crack his hard shell. To reveal his true nature, underneath the shy exterior. To help him reach his full potential, whatever that may be. To me, it couldn't be becoming a stuffy veterinarian and work with animals all day.

He was made for more.

I'd stopped toying with other guys, didn't even give them a sideways glance. I no longer would be shacking up with any man, no more robbing guys blind, no more parties for me. Instead, I'd started to find various girls who had a couch I could flop on for a spell. Even found a part-time job in the evenings when Bruce would be home on his beloved farm so I wouldn't miss a second with him. So okay, fine, I'd become a tiny bit responsible.

Because a girl's gotta have some cash for the basics. Food, clothes, ya know, essentials.

The job I ended up with turned out to be the perfect match for my particular skill set – seductress. It surprised me that there were opportunities out there where I could use my assets to their fullest. Without sinking to slimy depths as I had in the past. So wish I'd explored an avenue like this earlier, somehow though this hadn't ever crossed my mind as a good idea.

But picture this - a dive diner near a truck stop. Most of the customers were lonely men who were on the road for weeks at a time. Dingy beat-up blue formica tables with cracked and faded red vinyl bench seats. Steel trim on the grease-stained cream walls to match the steel exterior walls. Windows so caked with grime, they'd most likely never been washed since they'd been installed. Breakfast served all day, slimy chicken-fried steak as well.

The help wanted sign hung on the door stated they needed a waitress. One of the girls I crashed with at the time had mentioned the place to me. With a word of caution that no 'good' girl would dare set foot in a place like that. When I entered to ask about the job, the woman at the long front counter yelled "Hank!" over her shoulder and wandered off somewhere.

Hank emerged from the back, grease-splotted apron swinging from his neck. Shoes covered in flour dust. Faded black pants spotted with who knows what. Grayish white t-shirt, splotched with what looked like ketchup, mustard and other goo. Stainless steel spatula in hand being wielded as a weapon. His massive size resulted in his stomach wobbling like a bowl of jello.

"Yeah?" He barked, ogling me up and down.

Gulping down what felt like glass in my throat, I squeaked out, "The job?"

"You'll do." He spun awkwardly on his heels and waddled back into the kitchen.

No questions about my ability to hold a plate or to count change. Nothing at all. But, as I would soon learn, my appearance was way more important than my skills. The prettier the better.

The frilly blue outfit I had to wear at work I altered a bit to show off my cleavage better. Also shortened it a bit to give a one and all a better view of my legs as well. The little white apron I kept spotless. Which was no small feat considering how many times a day I put my hands in the front pocket. With a few winks, nods, hip wiggles, gentle touches, and the right word at the right time, I ended up with a mountain of tips. Almost as easy as picking pockets. Well, I did also receive more than a few offers for dates. Which I turned down flat.

I couldn't be stepping out on Bruce.

Because the funny thing was, my heart did this little flutter every time I saw Bruce or went anywhere near him. Every inch of me would tingle, I'd become all warm and flushed. When he touched me, I'd melt in more ways than one. And when he stalked off to go to class, a very large knife plunged into my chest, it hurt that much. In essence, I could only breathe when I was with him, despite the fact he left me light headed most of the time. He became my whole world, everything else hazy as I rushed through those hours just to return to him again.

Love. Could it be? No. I don't do that.

Things had gone too far, I'd pushed my luck and I no longer controlled anything. Things were racing down this road but I wasn't sure who was directing where anything was going. Chaos I could handle, but letting go of the steering wheel of my life I couldn't.

It was time to end this, whatever it was with Bruce. I came up with a sure-fire plan, a grand finale to our relationship. Then I'd head for somewhere else, anywhere else. Continue on as if nothing had happened here in Back Of Beyond, Texas. I'd blink, click my heels three times, and leave this place without a backward glance.

Forget Bruce. Even if I had to rip my heart out to do so.

For about two months, I'd been patient with Bruce. Trying to find a way to have him be alone with me, but that remained an elusive goal. We'd hang out on the quad, with half of the student body. We'd grab a bite at a diner, with a bunch of other students. We'd kiss, we'd flirt, we never did anything improper or anything even resembling that. Every time I thought we were drawing closer together, he'd pull back. For example, take the one time he dared to put his hand under my top. You'd thought he'd gotten burned on a hot stove because of how fast he pulled it back out.

And by November, I hadn't made much headway with Bruce. Nothing more than a few rather chaste kisses which did nothing more than cause him to blush from head to toe. Thus, I invented a birthday. Oh, I have a birthday of course, but it's in the spring not fall. Yet I didn't want to wait that long, this would give me the perfect excuse to force him to stretch himself. To step into manhood so to speak.

Deep inside me, my gut told me this is what he needed. Because this is what all of the other boys did with girls.

"Sweetie, next week is my birthday," I whispered in his ear, pressing against him tightly as we lounged on the grass next to the science building. I'd found him that day, nose-deep in a giant book as usual. I'd plopped the book on the ground beside him as I'd wiggled onto his lap.

"Wow, neat! We'll go out to dinner to celebrate." He gave me a quick peck on the cheek, leaning back a bit as he did so.

"How about you ask me what I want?" I smiled, warming to my plan of making this be his idea, opening my arms wide to embrace him and the whole wide world. Loving life, happy as I ever thought I could be.

"Okay, what do you want Donna?" Holding me as far out as he could without forcing me off his lap, he looked into my eyes, a slight grin on his face.

"I want us to spend the whole weekend together, somewhere other than here." I pushed back against his tight arms, snuggling against his chest, as I weaved my fingers in his coarse hair.

He gagged, he sputtered, his grip relaxed as he let go of me completely. I'd gotten more of a reaction then I'd ever dreamed I would. He coughed so hard he turned purple, not a great response. "Wha...?" he squeaked out as he dropped back onto the dark green grass, taking me with him as he did.

Giving him a moment to compose himself, I slid to the ground beside him. Watching his labored breathing, I sat up, still as a statue, pondering my next move. I wanted to stroke his arm but at that moment, fear filled me. *Had I taken things too far?*

No, we both needed to take this next step. Him more than me.

"Just the two of us, we never go anywhere private, are never alone, by ourselves. There's always so many people around." I swept my arm around to prove my point. "I need you all to myself for a change. Everyone else does things like that but us. We've been together forever. It's no big deal, honey." I shrugged my shoulders, tilting my head, pouting just a smidge. My outside calm, my inside raging. *What if he refuses?*

His eyes grew larger, his jaw clenched, the vein in his neck throbbed. Still, he didn't say a word.

"Get a motel room, dear." At this point I figured I needed to spell out what I meant by go somewhere to spend some time together. I helped him sit back up, patting him on the back a bit as I did.

"Not proper..." He looked to be at the point of panic.

"Nonsense, you live with your mother. I live on some random couch. A motel is the perfect place. We need to get to know each other better, more than just this little stuff we've already shared. It's my birthday and so picking the gift is up to me." I paused for a second. "And this is what I want." I tapped out each word with the tip of my finger on his chest. Best to leave things this way, a simple demand. I hoped he was getting excited. Or at least less freaked out.

"I don't think..." He looked like he'd had the biggest fright of his life, eyes wide open, mouth agape, sweat pouring off his forehead.

"Don't think, just do." I frowned. Running a finger down his face, I drew the outline of his lips with my fingernail. Ended up stroking the rough stubble along his jawline. Nothing I did ever worked with him, relaxation wasn't a word in his vocabulary most of the time. My mind raced with how to convince him to spend the weekend with me.

And I came up blank.

"No." Always with the single word answers, always tense, always so stiff.

"It's my birthday, my special day." Throwing him a pouty face. No more calm, soft, easy. I was going to have to throw myself at him right here in the middle of the quad. Debated for a split second about ripping off my top, but I kissed his hand instead. Then I began to move towards making a more intimate gesture as I slipped my hand onto his leg. But he shifted enough that we were no longer connected, no part of us were touching.

"Maybe." He jumped up quickly as lightning. Grabbing his backpack, he held it in front of his pants as he headed for anywhere but near me.

I haven't the faintest idea why he agreed in the end, it came as rather a shock when he called to tell me 'yes' the next day. Plans were set into motion, and I made my arraignments to ensure this moment would be special for him. I spent money I couldn't afford to waste on a lingerie set – pink and frilly. I got my hair done at a real salon, not by one of my friends. I primped every inch of me. Borrowed an overnight case from a friend, my backpack not being very ladylike and all.

What I didn't find out until our weekend getaway was that I would be his first. Yes, I'd had my suspicions based on his reactions and how little he'd touched me. However, the guilt on his face as we entered the dingy motel office confirmed this fact once and for all. He'd never even come close to being intimate with anyone.

As he interacted with the snobby clerk, fear filled me. So certain he'd turn tail and run. While he stood there, stiff as a board staring at that overly done up woman, he'd been rubbing his sweaty hand on his pants. Rather obvious he'd been trying to put up a brave front for me. But he'd used a fake name to register, not wishing anyone to know his business. Which had been so pointless given the rathole he'd picked. I'd stayed in better places when I'd been broke and in-between hippie groups.

No one would ever find out we were here unless we spilled the beans.

His hesitation when we entered the room should have made me stop and say 'never mind.' Yet I pressed on, because somehow, I thought making him be like me would make his life better. Free, easy, unconventional. Part of the counterculture, hippie crowd. No longer caring about what society thought we young people should or should not be doing.

Oh, how wrong I was.

Yes, I did manage to help him to loosen up a bit over the course of our two days in that motel. We barely came up for air. Hiding out in the room, taking a break only once the whole weekend. I went to find more food because I hadn't packed enough sandwiches for his voracious appetite. And I came to realize that I couldn't leave.

Not Texas. Not Bruce.

I now thought I understood a tiny bit about my mother and maybe why she'd stayed with Charles. Deep underneath all of the pain, she must've had feelings like I did at some point. Must've thought she could make him be kind if she just acted on those warm fuzzies. Had a connection to him that she couldn't undo any more than she could stop breathing.

When Bruce dropped me off on Sunday night, I stood in the bathroom. Staring at myself in the mirror, knowing everything had changed. My feelings I'd been trying to ignore and pretend were something else were, in fact, love. Bruce and I shared a bond that I'd never experienced with anyone else in my life before. And, unlike my mother, I'd picked a man who believed in family, in tradition, in kindness. He cared deeply about doing the right thing, not hurting others. On some level, I sensed he wanted what was best for me, to protect me.

He'd brought light into my dark world.

CHAPTER 7

New Mexico – Present Day

"And he didn't share those feelings of love? Or was he too guilty about everything?" Timothy began to ask, then hesitated for a moment. Standing up, he turned his back to me, leaning on the railing for a moment. He shifted his head up to look out towards the distant mountains. "Sorry Miss Donna, those questions may have been unfair to ask." He threw those words over his shoulder, a distinct catch in his throat.

"Don't worry, your words can't cause me more pain than my poor life choices already have. And please stop calling me 'Miss', you're making me feel old. Just 'Donna' will do fine. We're friends now." I untwisted from my cross-legged position on the swing, rising up on unsteady legs. One tingling, painful pins and needles as it awakened. I debated for a second about giving this boy a hug, but thought it might seem a bit improper. "I need a glass of water, you want one?"

He swung partially around, nodding his head but not speaking a word.

As I entered the small cabin that had become my refuge over the last few years, the thought crossed my mind again. Had Jenny found only me? Or had she found Bruce as well? Because wouldn't our child want to find both her parents? How hard had it been for her? After all these years, how do you even begin to search for someone? Especially when you don't even have something as basic as their name to go on? When I'd found Stan, it hadn't been overly difficult. However, I had several key bits of the puzzle before I'd entered even one word into the search bar.

My poor child might have been hunting for answers most of her life.

I busied myself for a moment. Gathering bread, cheese, cutting fuji apple slices, filling glasses with water. I hadn't changed my vegan dietary habits much from back in the day when I roamed the earth in pink buses. At restaurants I often didn't have a choice. Eat normal food with normal people. All because the menu selections were so limited when you chose not to eat animal products. And I never wanted to attract attention by asking a laundry list of questions. Does this have butter, cheese? Or about other ingredients that might be hidden in certain items. I rolled with it, and the guilt of eating some poor animal.

But when I cooked for myself, I went down the road of depravity. Thus, the cheese I now stood cutting wasn't real, some rubbery substance made from soy that tasted like feet. The bread I'd made myself, sprouted grains with a pinch of herbs which wasn't horrible. Both were as fake as I was.

My diet, one of many self-inflicted punishments. Not getting close to people was another.

Pushing memories down, I ignored visions of what Bruce might be like now. If he had survived, came home in one piece, got married, had kids. Or if he'd died in a rice paddy somewhere. Or if, in fact, it'd all been bluster and he'd never enlisted at all. He'd stayed right there in Texas. Finished school, became a veterinarian and helped farm animals from sunup to sundown. Married some farm girl, lived on a farm, had a bunch of farm kids.

In the end, did it matter much? I'd seen his face that day. I'd taken his good natured, kind hearted soul and ripped it out of his chest. Then I'd stomped on it before throwing it in the garbage heap with all the other debris I'd left in my wake over the years.

Guilt, so much guilt.

Putting everything on a serving tray, along with two plates, I returned to the porch. Timothy pulled open the screen door for me when I approached with my hands full, such a polite young man. Setting down my burden, I plopped into one of the chairs at the outdoor table on the far side of the porch. Timothy joined me on the opposite side. We munched in silence for a few moments. Companions for a flash of time, equals.

"Vietnam." I murmured.

"What?" This word muffled, a bite of apple half-eaten in his mouth.

"The reason Bruce and I didn't end up together." Not exactly, but it was the simple answer. And the way I'd justified and vilified Bruce for years.

"Oh…" He set down the piece of apple, placing his hands flat on the table, fingers spread wide. Nibbling on his lower lip, he squinted his eyes, deep in thought. He nodded his head, snapped his fingers, he'd had a eureka moment. "He got drafted!"

"No, he didn't wait for that to happen." I took a long drink of water, swallowing hard to keep my heart from jumping out of my chest. The intense anguish from that moment so long ago, still hitting me even now. When Bruce had said he'd rather fight in a war than be with me. "Or at least I don't think he did."

He munched on the snack for a while, deep in thought. "I wonder what kind of unanswered questions my birth parents have. I mean, there must be a few."

"My gut instinct would be that those are more about you than about each other." I patted his hand resting on the side of his plate, my crystal pinky ring hitting the glass on the tabletop as I did. The chime echoed for a second, then I rapped my ring again. The sound soothed me for some reason.

"You know it's rather easy to look up Veterans who were killed in Vietnam. Because of the memorial." He pushed his plate off to the side, shifting a bit in his seat so he could pull out his slim phone from his back pocket. "What's Bruce's last name?"

My heart stopped, the air came out of my lungs in a rush. Did I want to find out that answer? After all of this time was I prepared to face the truth of what might have been the end result of the rashness of youth? Before I could even think, the name popped out of my mouth. Watching in horror, my eyes widened as Timothy's thumbs typed madly on the phone.

He gave me a quick peep, and his hands stilled. "Oh, sorry, Donna. I shoulda asked first. But when you said the guy's name, I figured everything was good. My bad. I'll put it away, I can see you're not okay with this."

Yet the ache in me said otherwise, this little piece of information I had to have as much as I needed air, water and food. "No, tell me if he's listed." I gulped, trying not to throw up. "Please."

He fiddled with his phone for a moment more. "Nope, not listed." Setting the phone down, he held out his hand. "You cool with that?"

I wasn't sure. That led to more questions than answers as far as I could tell. "I guess for now, it will have to do." I gave his hand a bit of a squeeze, giving my head a small shake. But inside, every inch of me was being jolted by an intense tingling sensation. I tightened every muscle, squeezing every part of myself hard. Holding my breath as I contemplated the meaning of what I'd just learned. "It doesn't tell us much now does it?"

Bruce might very well be alive and well, living out there somewhere.

Did some small part of me still love him? I didn't have any idea. However, the fact remained, he'd been the one person I'd ever become close to, had any kind of a connection with. Would I still melt, have those sparks ignite my soul if I saw him again? No. Too much had happened, too many things which couldn't be undone.

Did he ever think about me? About us? About the baby?

As much as I'd tried to block that period of my life from popping into my head, it so often did. More about my child and what had happened to him or her after the birth. No, I'd never dreamed of the white picket fence life. That had never been in my future, never been my destiny.

But our child, yes, I'd dreamed about our child often.

Was he a strong, sturdy boy like Bruce? Was he stern, prone to looking at life with a practical eye, set in his ways? Did he have brown hair, deep, dark brown eyes? Or was she like me? Wispy, willowy, floating along in life. Was she a tiny little thing with blonde hair like me? With these weird eyes that changed colors? Or had he or she gotten a mix of the two of us? Over the years, my image of this imaginary child had shifted, morphed, never settling on one thing.

Because I had nothing to go on.

One thing I had come to learn, it wasn't easier to forget simply because I hadn't ever even laid eyes on my child. That lie I'd been told had never sat well with me. While I hadn't even spoken about my child out loud until now, I'd held her close to my heart. Yes, there were days I'd tried to push those thoughts out of my head. Bruce I could forget. Our child, it wasn't possible to.

He nodded, "If he went, he came home. If he didn't go, there's no way of knowing for sure. I'm sorry, I wish there was a way to find out more."

I remained still, unable to move past the weight of all of this as so many thoughts tumbled into my mind.

"So, okay, let's say your Bruce did go. How'd he end up there if he wasn't drafted? I don't think my history teacher ever said anything about anyone going there willingly." He tapped on the table, causing everything to bounce on the unsteady surface. "Well, not like we really learned much about that war. Mostly we learned about World War I and World War II. Guess Vietnam is too unpopular to even teach to high school kids these days." Tim jumped into the silence, eager to further the conversation. "I mean, you don't have to fill me in on all the details if you don't want to or anything."

Hello old friend regret, this one is on me. If in fact, Bruce had enlisted that is. "No, it's fine, Tim." I sniffed the fresh air for a second, composing myself before diving in. "I backed him into a corner." I stood up, moving back to my more comfortable spot on the swing. "He couldn't handle being a father. No, scratch that. He couldn't handle me."

CHAPTER 8

Texas – 1968

By the beginning of February, it became rather clear I'd made a colossal mistake. One I couldn't fix, undo, or erase. I debated about going to some clinic or doctor for verification. But figured in this small of a town, tongues would wag. Everyone would end up spreading my business as the best new bit of gossip before the sun had set. This particular secret had to be held close for as long as possible, shared with only one other person.

My initial idea had been to wait until Valentine's Day to fill Bruce in on the details of my little dilemma. We'd been planning a special day together, just the two of us. At first, I'd hope we'd have a repeat of our weekend at the motel. Only somewhere a bit nicer this second time. But once I'd figured out my little dilemma, I stopped pushing for that. Happy we were doing anything together at all.

However, in the end, my nerves got the best of me. My anxiety levels wouldn't allow me to continue walking on the edge that long. Each time I'd look at Bruce, my stomach would clench. My head swimming with the knowledge that I was about to change our lives forever. No longer did I gaze at him and want to rip his clothes off no matter where we might happen to be.

Or maybe those feelings were nothing more than the morning sickness.

Thus, a few days early, after another restless night I decided 'today is the day.' I marched right over to him on the quad and insisted we go somewhere to talk, in private. No one else could hear the words I needed to speak. Girls didn't get themselves in trouble and then shout the news for all and sundry to hear.

Sliding into his truck that morning, somehow my heart sensed I'd never be with Bruce again after this moment. An aching longing so deep filled me, every part of me hurt. These few months, no, he still had years, should have remained precious. His life was still so sacred, innocent, unmarred. As he walked into manhood, became who he was destined to be, learned who he was, broke out of the shadow of his family. The last thing he needed right now had to be a family of his own, I'd be a burden, a liability. I'd stop him from reaching his full potential, from achieving his dreams.

I'd been so foolish to think otherwise.

And a big part of me didn't want to tell him about my pregnancy. To pretend this chat was about something else, then leave him wondering why I'd disappeared. Not like he wasn't aware I'd drifted in from somewhere and would wander off at some point. Nothing more than an autumn leaf which had fully changed and would now blow away in the winter wind.

I remained silent as he parked the truck in the shade under a grove of trees on a river bank. Something changed as I gazed into his questioning face. I had to say something, I had to do what was right. Not just for him but for me and the child I now carried. But for the life of me, I couldn't figure out what that might be. I'd miscounted the days, and ended up picking the wrong weekend for my fake birthday. How I'd managed to mix things up, I wasn't quite clear on. Up to this point, my record had been flawless. Not even one moment of held breath for a few late days, I knew my body and my rhythm.

Thus, the mistake made had been mine alone. I couldn't lay this at Bruce's feet.

Taking in a cleansing breath, I squeezed my eyes shut tight for a moment before opening them again. "I love you. With all my heart and soul, Bruce, I've grown to love you. I didn't expect that. Did you?" I glanced over at him, tilting my head a little, not wanting to look him in the eye.

He hesitated, unsure how to respond. "Sure baby. I've been having fun with you."

I grimaced, *fun*, that's all I amount to? But I didn't take the bait. He reached out his hand, I pulled myself deeper into the corner of the seat. Not wanting to share even a second of intimacy with him ever again. Understanding how weak I'd be if I allowed myself to love him in the fullness of that word. I slammed shut the door of my heart. Forcing myself to grow cold and distant.

"I love you too." His words, forced and awkward.

Gnawing on my bottom lip, my thoughts raged, my fingernail tracing the paisley print on the skirt of my dress. "I'm pregnant." The words popped out, almost of their own volition. I hadn't wanted to go there before, even less now that thing had turned so weird.

And he went into a bit of a tizzy. Swatting at things, breathing hard. Fists clenched as he lowered his head and spat out words of blame towards me. As if I hadn't already figured out I'd messed up, miscalculated things and ruined everything. The instant I'd figured out my dilemma, I should've run and never looked back. This moment with Bruce shouldn't be happening, another error on my part. He'd have been better off if I'd left him in the dark wondering why I'd left and where I'd gone. So much better than torturing him like this. I'd destroyed the only thing in my world worth anything.

Because good boys don't do things like this, get girls in the family way. And Bruce was so much more than a good boy.

The conversation became tit for tat, neither of us wanting to give an inch. Each of us driving a wedge between us deeper and deeper with each word spoken. We'd started the day being a few steps apart and ended up an ocean apart. With no way to build a bridge that strong or that long.

Somewhere deep inside of me I'd breathed a silent wish for the fairytale. I'd wanted the impossible. The house with the white picket fence, this man by my side forever as we raised this child in perfect harmony. Happy, safe, secure. Protected from the outside world in our blissful, perfect little bubble.

But we didn't live in that world. No, scratch that. I don't live in that world, Bruce did.

I was nothing more than a homeless drifter walking on the clouds. He had his feet planted firmly on the ground and had a better grasp of the bottomless hole we'd fallen into. He understood his standing as a young man who could be called to play the part of a cog in the war machine at any time. He'd often told me that the only reason he studied so hard was to avoid the draft. A wife and baby didn't fit into that, we'd be too much added pressure. An unnecessary burden added to his already heavy load. He'd crumble under the weight.

He understood this as much as I did.

"I'll join the army. I hear the hazard pay from the war isn't half bad. Send you some money so you don't have to worry." His whole body cold, stiff. Like the first day we'd met.

"No!" This couldn't be about money. That's what it had been for my mother in the end, she'd married Charles because he'd been the one with the most cash. Bruce and I had so much more, I needed to cling to that belief. But there wasn't any way to explain this to him without revealing more about myself than I ever wished to. "You can't do something hateful like that, it'd undo all the love we share!" I spat out the one thing I could think of that would be close enough to the truth to still make my point.

He prattled on with reason after reason why he had to leave as I gripped his arm as tight as I could. Trying to hold onto the one thing I had in this life, the only real, honest, good thing I'd ever had. As my heart shattered, I let go. And accepted that we weren't meant to be. I screamed something trivial in response about love and hate. Giving him an out, an excuse to push me even further away.

Yet, one little bit of me still wanted my child to have everything, a Father and Mother. Even if we weren't the greatest couple on the planet. "Stay here and do what's right..." But too much anger had passed before these words and I shrank into the seat in defeat. We were over, my little spot of happiness I'd found had been destroyed.

I shouldn't have allowed my temper to get the best of me, I shouldn't have been upset with Bruce for his response to my news. We both should've walked away and come back to the discussion another day. However, we were young and impetuous. And I flat out didn't know any better. This is how my mother and Charles appeared to solve all of their differences. A drunken yelling match that ended with her being beaten to a bloody pulp.

At least neither of us had any visible wounds.

In the end, my gut told me he would follow through on his threat to enlist. He was a man of his word and didn't toss out ideas wildly. There didn't seem to be any reason for me to stick around for a second longer. My best move appeared to be catching the next bus to anywhere but here.

No, I didn't feel the need to fill Bruce in on my plans. We'd screamed ourselves hoarse in those few minutes we sat in his truck. There didn't seem to be any point to adding anything else to the argument. Or to further widen the massive divide that now lay between us. Best to leave things as they were. Broken into so many pieces that most had become lost. Where they would become so deeply buried they could never be found.

On the ride back into town, I ignored the music blaring out of the radio. Which I do believe had been a signal from Bruce he didn't want to continue the conversation either. Instead, I plotted my next move.

Literally. Few options remained, I hadn't saved much from my few nights working at the diner. And yes, there had been a few babies among the groups I'd been wondering around the country with over the past few years. However, those children didn't seem to be well cared for. They were often raised by everyone and anyone without much thought as to who the parents might be.

Not to mention the fact that most of these groups were anti-war. There were protests and marches, which came with threats of being arrested at any moment. Plus, all of the drugs and alcohol being passed around much of the time. Sure the music events were fun. Still they tended to be party scenes with so much debauchery that in my mind, no child should ever be near.

None of what I'd been doing since I'd fled my broken home had been much better. Not the types of environments I wanted for my baby at all. I had such grand hopes and dreams for my child. Flashes over the few weeks since I'd discovered my predicament that I would conjure up. Knowing none of it would happen, hoping it would anyway. I didn't have anywhere to go, but I couldn't stay here a second longer.

I had one door left open to me. I'd have to slink back home to my mother with my tail between my legs.

CHAPTER 9

New Mexico – Present Day

"Oh, Donna. Wow. I don't know what to even say to you at this point." Timothy slapped the armrest of the Adirondack chair.

How had I missed the fact he'd move from the table to there? "You don't need to add anything to this little tale. I made so many mistakes as a teenager, but yes, this is why when you started to search for Bruce's name, well…"

He flicked his fingers for a moment. Squinting his eyes as he considered the ramifications of what I'd shared. "Maybe my birth parents were like you and Bruce. All it took was one fight to break up. Then, boom, I'm handed over to strangers." He stared at me, wanting to make sense of his world. To get answers from the wrong person.

I picked at an imaginary itch at the corner of my eye for a second or two as I debated how best to respond. "I guess that's one possible scenario, but I do believe you shouldn't jump to conclusions. I'm fairly sure there's lots of other explanations. Your birth Mother might have believed she wasn't the best person to be your full time caregiver. Or a million other reasons. If you do ever connect with her, don't walk into that conversation with preconceived ideas. Especially if those notions are based on my rather bad example of life."

He twisted his head, gazing first at the floor then upwards towards the beams of the ceiling. "To be honest, I was kinda running away this morning. I was supposed to be cleaning a rental for a check-in this afternoon. Instead, I stormed off, planned on taking the path," his chin pointed towards the trail that winds behind my cabin off into the distance. "If Mom isn't my mom, why should I keep doing all of this dumb stuff for her? Not like she pays me. Well, not much anyway." He grunted.

I wanted to scream, *'Because she's put a roof over your damn head for nineteen years! Don't be a brat!'* But I didn't, that wouldn't be fair. Based on my own relationship with my mother, I had no right to be telling anyone to make nice with theirs. But I now understood why he'd been so insistent earlier about finding out if I'd reached out to my mother. I didn't know if he'd meant after I'd fled the scene as a kid. Or at some later point in time. But the when did matter. Because that question hadn't been about me at all.

"Uhm, maybe you should let her know you ended up here instead." I didn't want to hurt Carol by having her think that I didn't understand the value of Timothy's time. But given what little I'd heard about what his heart and mind wrestled with at this moment, he did need a day off.

He let out a little cough, "Oh, trust me she knows where I am as long as I have my phone."

That I didn't even begin to comprehend one tiny little bit. Did he mean she could call him at any point so she didn't need to worry? I wasn't sure. However, given the level of confidence in which he'd uttered this statement, I sensed it would be best to leave it alone.

"Okay. But I'm going to throw your words from before back at you Tim. Carol is your mother. She deserves to learn from you what you're struggling with right now. And why you're not doing okay." I give him a hint of a smile. "And believe me when I say, running away doesn't really solve anything."

He squinted his eyes, as he began to crack his knuckles one by one.

"Which is why you went back home when you got pregnant."

It had come time to rip off another band aid and expose a wound that hadn't healed in over fifty years. "I meant what I said before. That wasn't possible, we'd both been in places in our lives where there wasn't a way to build a bridge back to each other. I had to make my own way in life. And I fell flat on my face, failing at everything."

CHAPTER 10

Texas - Illinois 1968

When Bruce stopped to drop me off, I jumped out, slamming the door behind me. Not caring in the least that he gunned the engine the second I'd stepped onto the sidewalk. Nor that he'd left a cloud of smoke in his wake. I marched into the small house I'd been crashing at for a few months. Stuffed what little I owned into my backpack and walked over to the bus depot. Bought a one-way ticket back to my hometown. But, by Dallas, the heat of my anger had cooled. I stepped off the bus, grabbed my pack and walked into the terminal, scanning the area for a payphone booth.

With butterflies in my stomach, my clammy hands dialed the operator. I did so many deep breaths waiting to be connected that I became light headed and faint. It took forever for my party to finally be connected over the staticky line.

"Hello?" My mother's voice, the same as I remembered it even after all these years, husky, slinky, sultry. Designed to attract all of the wrong kind of attention. Didn't matter that she'd netted herself a husband years ago.

"Mom, it's me, Donna, your daughter." Not sure why I added that last bit, she only had one daughter. Well, for all I knew that is. She and Charles might've had a bunch more kids after I'd taken off.

A loud cough on line, silence, another cough, but no reply.

"Hello? Hello? Are you still there Mom?" I leaned against the glass wall, the coolness feeling like ice against my flushed face.

"Yes, I'm here. Wha' ya' want?" She snarled, so unlike her.

"I'm on my way back, thought you should know before I show up. Didn't want to just drop in unannounced. I'll be there in a few days." I started to tap on the metal shelf below the large dark phone with a fingernail. The tinging sound ringing in the enclosed space, but I didn't stop.

"Ya can't. Chuck don't have but one kid. And you ain't it." She coughed again.

"I'm pregnant." Appeared to me that my best plan had to be keeping things simple, straightforward. A level she'd understand, because she'd been there.

"Marry the guy like I done." She huffed, "Broken bones are the price you pay to have a roof over ya head." Click. She'd hung up on me.

Yup, my mother had stuck it out with Charles, who now had a nickname apparently. And from the sounds of things, their relationship had remained abusive. But I hadn't fallen in love with a man who hurt me. However, I'd burned my bridges and couldn't go back to Bruce even if he hadn't gone through on his rash plan to enlist.

Still clutching the phone receiver, staring up at the dark ceiling, tears filled my eyes. I couldn't even form one image of what to do next. How could I care for a baby on my own? Scraping up enough money to keep me fed hadn't been easy and who would hire me when I started to look like a hippo? A rap on the door of the booth startled me out of my reverie, I needed a plan, a place to go, a place to hide.

Grabbing my stuff, head hung low, I shuffled past the man waiting to use the phone. Turning my head this way and that, I give a quick scan of the other waiting passengers. Not surprised in the least that most of them were young men in uniform. These poor draftees here everywhere, being called up against their will. Being sent off to a war they didn't believe in, didn't want to fight in. My generation would be forever shaped by this moment in history.

And I didn't care in the least.

Out past the idling buses I went, in the end this place was as good as anywhere else I could've landed. I marched down the streets of Dallas, not seeing anything, not caring about anything. Tomorrow I would figure out life. Today, I needed to wallow in self pity. Not bothering to wipe my face, I continued to weep, soft cries as I grieved the loss of the one thing I'd ever wanted.

Love.

When my blistered feet could carry me no more, I ended up discovering a little rooming hotel to hide out in for a while. Found myself another bad job as a waitress. Fewer tips, because I no longer flirted my way through life. Yet I managed to earn enough that I was good for a while, saving as much as I could for when my time came. Dull, quiet existence for a few months as I floated along, just holding on as my life fell apart.

Then another bus trip. After trading my backpack for a suitcase because it would be easier to use in my present state. For this trip, it didn't matter where I ended up, I'd worn out my welcome in Dallas. A few people were starting to ask questions that I couldn't answer. Yes, I could've lied, spun some tale about a dead husband. Lots of girls were being left widowed from the war. Don't think anyone would have given it a second thought even without a ring on my finger.

But I was done with being fake, not being honest, not living in the truth of the moment.

However, even my oversized dresses weren't doing the trick to hide my ever growing belly. And the grumbles and out and out disrespectful remarks were getting to me. I'd bought a ticket to St. Louis after my last shift. But because I'd worked all day and was seven months pregnant, I fell asleep the instant the bus had started to move. The gentle rocking movement had lulled me into a deep slumber, nestled deep in my seat in the rear. Nothing disturbed me as the coach rambled along the highways northward.

"Miss, you have to depart now. It's the end of the line." Gruff voice, booming into my sleeping brain.

As I peeled my eyes open, I rubbed them to make the world be a little less hazy. Nodding, unable to say much, I peeped up at the large, doughy, red-faced man. His wrinkled uniform hugged his chest. The silver buttons strained trying not to pop off from the pressure. Rising, I snagged my pack from where I'd stashed it at my feet. As I followed him off the bus, I realized I wasn't sure where I'd landed and that I didn't really care as long as it wasn't Dallas.

Walking into the station, I found the first available wooden bench. Plopping down, placing my junk at my feet and wrapping my arms around me to hide the obvious. My stomach rumbled, when was the last time I'd eaten? Not sure. How long had I been asleep? Not sure about that either. My eyes dimmed as I stared off into the distance, looking at nothing. I contemplated my rather poor life choices which had led me to this moment.

"You look a bit lost, dear." With no warning, a soft hand squeezed my shoulder.

Turning my head, I gave the woman standing next to me the once over. A nun, prim and proper in her dark habit, had somehow ended up at my side. How had I missed that? "Where are we?" I pressed my lips together, "I fell asleep on the bus." For some reason I didn't want her to think I was stupid.

"Chicago." Direct and to the point as she patted my arm and sat beside me. "I'm Sister Ann."

Well, this was as good as anywhere, I guess. She dug in her large tote bag, pulling out sandwiches wrapped in wax paper. She handed me one, then rewrapped the rest. "Thanks," I mumbled as I took a bite. "I'm Donna."

"Where are you trying to go? I'll see if I can find you the right bus since you missed your stop." Her eyes twinkled; her face warm as she rubbed my back.

Hesitating, I tried to frame an answer. "I guess here. To be honest, I don't have anywhere to go. I broke up with my boyfriend months ago and my mother told me not to come home." I swallowed hard, the food I'd just eaten tasting sour as I choked a bit and bile rose. My truth shouldn't be told.

A wave washed over her face, changing it from friendly to fierce. "You got yourself in trouble." Simple enough of a statement but these words spoke volumes.

Placing the half-eaten sandwich on my lap, I shook my head, too ashamed to give an answer out loud to a stranger.

She pursed her lips. "You will come with me, we will take care of you and you will put the child up for adoption." Not a question, not a suggestion, a demand. "It's what's best, dear. Trust me."

Oh how I wish I'd run the other way.

Instead, I listened to her prattle on about those other 'lost lambs' her group helped. For about an hour before her bus boarded she never let up. Meek as a kitten, I followed her onto the bus, off the bus and into a waiting car once we'd arrived at her home city. Not really questioning anything. Thankful I didn't have to figure out anything. Grateful she's promised me a place to stay for a while at least.

But the part about giving up my baby didn't sit well with me, I'd been stewing on that ever since she's mentioned it. This baby and I were going to face the world together. No matter what. When we arrived at the large building, I guess I was surprised by the size of it. Don't know why, but I had pictured a real home in my head, not an institution.

There was a moment of whispering among the nuns, then Sister Ann led me to a room. "We'll talk more in the morning."

The stark white room held nothing more than two small beds and a dresser, which was more than enough for me. Plain faded pink gingham curtains on the lone window. Pale pink chintz spreads on the twin beds.

Worn whitewash on the small dresser.

The sun hadn't begun to shine through the window when a knock came at the door, "Time for morning prayers."

Dressing quickly, I peeped around to see where I should be going. A few other young women were shuffling down the hall, I followed them. A few waddled, much later in their pregnancies than me, all remained silent, heads bowed. We sat in a long room behind the sisters. No one spoke, the prayers were quiet reveries. I stared at the pictures hung on the walls, wondering if they were saints. A bell rang. Everyone rose and began to leave.

We walked into another room, smells of burnt eggs and bacon hit my nose, making me gag. I followed the line and received my breakfast plate, a few bits of soft chatter had begun to fill the room. Finding a spot in a far corner, I perched on my chair, a silent witness to everything and everyone around me. There were six nuns in total. About twenty of us that I took to be guests like me, in various stages of showing. Most worrisome of all, the two women who served breakfast were both obviously pregnant. Thus, it would appear at some point I'd be put to work doing something. This offer wasn't an act of charity by a kindly nun.

No free lunch here, and I wasn't sure what game they were playing.

As others finished, dishes were scraped into the waiting trash bin. Then placed on a passthrough window shelf looking into the kitchen area. I got a glimpse of the woman washing them, unsure if I'd seen her eating breakfast. The others had for the most part wandered out of the dining area. I continued to watch as the lone stragglers took their sweet time finishing their meals.

As I continued rooted in my spot unsure what to do, a nun approached me. "Follow me."

Rising, my footsteps matched hers the short way down a corridor to a small office. She nestled in behind a large desk, prim and proper with her hands folded in front of her. No other chair had been placed in the room. I stood before her, awkward and uncomfortable, as I shifted from one foot to the other. She bowed her head for a few moments, eyes closed, leaving me to wait as my frustration at the situation mounted.

I'd become a child called to the principal's office about to be scolded and punished for doing something wrong.

Seconds before I would've snapped out something rude, her head came back up. Her eyes bored into me, taking in every bit of me, inside and out. "I'm Sister Marie. And, well, dear, seems you've gotten yourself in a bit of a mess. But that's why we're here."

Mess? That didn't appear to be quite the right word to use. Yet the effort required for making an argument here, didn't seem worth it. "Well, I need some help getting myself settled, finding a place. Maybe a job that doesn't require me to stand on my feet all day. Then me and the baby will be good."

"Oh Donna, you will not keep the baby dear. No man will ever want you if you do. You don't want to be known as that kind of woman, now do you?" She grimaced. "No man may ever want you ever again as it is because of this," she waved a finger towards my stomach. "Which is why it's best no one knows you're here. Thus, we don't allow visitors, or phone calls, or letters. Do you understand?" Her dark eyes matched the dark cloth of her habit, she narrowed them into slits as she stared at me. The ice from her attitude could've frozen me solid from a million miles away. "Not to mention that baby will be much better off with a Father and a Mother." She placed heavy emphasis on 'Father.' It was clear who she believed to be more important person in this equation. "A child needs a good, solid, stable home. You would never be able to provide that."

Did I have no say in the matter? Rather clear that the answer to this was 'no.' I nodded my head. Saying a word might give her more ammo against me. Because, while she hadn't said it in so many words, I sensed her condemnation, her disapproval, her hatred. Those snide half comments had spoken volumes. Shame washed over me as I lowered my head. This would forever be how people viewed me if they would ever learn the truth about my pregnancy. Not as a hippy who believed in free love. But as a woman who couldn't keep her legs together.

"Later today you'll be given your assignments and we'll give you an examination to see how healthy the baby is." A mocking tone in her voice, to her it couldn't be possible I'd be carrying a child worthy of anything.

Again, I gave a small shake of my head. Not wishing to agree with the woman but not wishing to disagree either.

"Dismissed." She waved a hand towards the door.

I tiptoed out, and continued to walk with as light a step as I could back to my assigned room. Sinking onto the flimsy mattress, my heart sank. I had maybe a few hundred bucks in my purse despite all my hard work over the last few months. No way to live on that for long.

I'd been backed into a corner from which I didn't see a way out. Bruce should've been excited about my news. He should've wanted to take me home to his mother. Me being in this awful place was his fault. He'd been angry. He'd started the fight. He declared he'd rather go off to war than have this child.

Because of Bruce's actions I had nothing and nowhere else to go but here.

Curling into a small ball, I rocked back and forth as I grieved the loss of everything good that I'd ever had. Which wasn't much when I really thought about it. There had been one thing in my life that had been worth anything. Bruce. I missed his sweet smile, his innocence. His willingness to learn and grow. His ability to love without strings.

And I'd forced him to do something he wasn't ready for.

Rubbing my stomach, I whispered, 'I'm sorry.' Over and over again as the tears began to flow. I'd failed my baby, every inch of me painfully aware that in the end the blame here was mine and mine alone. My entire life had been nothing more than one mistake leading to another one. Heck, I couldn't even count out the days of the month properly which is how I'd gotten myself in this fix to begin with.

But Bruce still should've stepped up, acted like a man and done what was right.

A knock on the door broke my depressive thoughts for the moment. Swiping at my damp face as best I could with the sheets, I tried to smooth out the wrinkles in my massive dress. "Yes?" I called with a catch in my throat.

The door swung open to reveal Sister Ann.

CHAPTER 11

New Mexico – Present Day

"That doesn't seem fair." Timothy's words startled me.

I'd been so deep into my memories of those few months before my baby's birth that I'd been lost in them. Feeling those movements, flutters and kicks. Dreaming of what I wanted for this child as if I were still that young woman. All the things I would miss out on because I could never be this child's Mother. The norms that society had required something else of me, demanded I be something I wasn't. Pure, unsullied, wholesome. I'd have to give this child to a stranger and hope for the best.

"What?" I choked out, making a feeble attempt to swipe at the moisture on my face. Adults shouldn't sob in front of kids, right?

"That you didn't have any say in what happened to your baby. That's not true, is it? I mean, in the end, you made the decision, right?" He leaned forward in the chair opposite me, worry etched on his face.

"It was a different time back then. Each day someone made sure to remind me of how much of a 'mistake' I'd made. Of how 'bad' I was for getting myself in trouble. And how much better off the child would be in a 'good' home. These words eroded my self-confidence, erased my ability to see my own worth. I left that place broken and more alone than I'd ever been." I'd made sure to use air quotes around the important words. To make sure Tim understood the intense pressure I had endured back then.

But I didn't mention the walls around my heart a million miles high I'd built with these stones thrown at me. And then lived within that fortress for years. All because I never wanted anyone to come close enough to ever treat me that way again.

I caressed the soft yarn stitching of the bright orange knitted blanket on my lap. Wondering for maybe the millionth time if this child had received the things I made. If Jenny had been told where they had come from, if she in fact had them. What other green outfit could she be referring to but mine? Somehow she had been given my gift and was aware of the story behind it. No small miracle that was.

He chewed on a thumbnail, pondering my words. "Okay, what you're saying is that my birth Mother had options. That she willingly put me into the arms of my mother. Because she wouldn't have been told what you were told. And she could have raised me as a single Mother." He wrinkled his nose as he stared straight at me.

I didn't wish to go down a very dark rabbit hole, but a rather important point needed to be made here. "She had a much more fundamental choice to make, Tim. Life or death. That route wasn't open to me. Thus, major props to her for looking at all sides and then carrying you for months before giving you up. For saying, 'I think my child should go to a family with a Mom and a Dad. I believe that's what's best, for me and for my baby.' In the end she held all of the cards, no one else." I tried to match his gaze, but this became too much for me. My eyes began to well. I looked off at a wandering cloud far on the horizon for a second before flicking a quick peep back over at him.

"Oh." He scratched his forehead, and I regretted having put this thought into his mind. That he might not even be here at all. If his birth Mother had made a very different decision rather early on in her pregnancy, no baby. "What would you have done if abortion had been available?" I guess something on my face changed because he was quick to follow up with, "Sorry, that's way too personal for me to ask. Don't answer that."

"Don't ever be sorry for speaking from your heart." I swallowed hard, my throat dry. I loved that little thing growing inside of me from the first moment I sensed something might be off. "I wouldn't have changed a thing. She's the only good thing I've ever done with my life and I'm glad I had her." Hindsight's twenty-twenty. However, one fact remained, there were so many events and decisions in my life I should've done differently. And there's no do-overs in life, only the slow crawl towards our inevitable death.

But my child was one regret I didn't have. I would've carried her and given birth to her no matter what.

"So, are you going to call her like she wants?" His face emanated a small spark, a way to solve my problem and his. Because if I had the courage to reach out then surely he could do the same with his newly discovered birth Mother.

And now we'd arrived at what I'd been doing my level best to avoid all day. Jenny. Picking at a loose stitch in the blanket, I watched it start to unravel. Same as my life appeared to be doing right at this moment. "I'm not sure. You haven't heard everything about me, I've been rather selective with what I've chosen to share. I'm not who she's been looking for, not in the 'Mother' sense at least. I'm not worthy of the title, not even a little bit. Giving birth to someone doesn't make you a 'Mother.' Being there for the bumps and bruises of life does." I pulled a bit more on the yarn, regretting it the moment I did so. The blanket now had a rather large hole in it. "Which is why you need to give Carol a bit of slack. I think she did what she did because she believed, right or wrong, it was what was best for you."

He started to rise, changed his mind and sank back down. "I'm not sure I agree with you about my mom. But, I don't think what you've done with your life will matter much to your daughter." He touched the tip of his nose. "I always wondered why I didn't look much like my parents, thought it might be some weird genetic quirk. It wasn't. And now, I want to stare into the face of someone who looks like me." He took in a massive breath. "Most people don't understand. My buddies used to laugh at me when I would mention it. But I was jealous about them looking like someone in their family. Maybe you don't realize what a big deal that is either. But maybe that's all she wants too. To finally see someone who looks like her."

I'd been looking at this whole situation from my side of the glass, the dirt and the smudges I'd created on the window of life. But there was always another side. How did Jenny see this? While I'm sure there was a layer of anger and resentment, there just might be something else there. Something more driving her need to connect. But my pain still colored even that little bit of hope she didn't want to scream at me for abandoning her.

"There's one problem with that." I wagged a finger at him.

"What's that?" He lifted his eyebrows, leaning forward in anticipation of my answer.

"She's old enough to be from the era where she'd have been taught that I never wanted her." I slapped my thigh, sure that hatred had to be the main focus for my child. "Or worse, that good girls kept their legs shut and she'd know what kind of girl I was. Sorry for being so blunt there."

"Yet she still reached out." He gave me a wicked grin.

He had me there. "But she's not going to like the answers I'm going to give." Because all of me was a hot mess.

"Do you know how many questions I have formed in my mind in just the last twenty-four hours? And she's had a lifetime to work on those. I kinda don't think she's going to let you wiggle out of this."

"You do realize until she found me I didn't even know if I'd given birth to a boy or a girl?" I pushed my fingers into the void I'd created in the blanket, ready to deal with that part of the story.

CHAPTER 12

Illinois – 1968

For those couple of months before I gave birth, I followed all of the rules. Worked the tasks I was given. All while I watched and felt my child grow inside me. At each little flutter I became both ecstatic and weepy. My emotions so hard to control, knowing what lay ahead for both of us. I would have little conversations with this tiny being. Sending it good thoughts at various times during the day. At times I thought it might be a boy because it seemed so strong. At other times I wanted it to be a girl because I wished for it to look like me.

Boy or girl didn't matter, in the end, this child would never be mine.

Most of all, I wanted this child to have a life filled with love. The type I'd been given for those brief moments with Bruce. His kindness, his compassion, his graciousness. While I'd never met his mother, she'd raised him to be a good, honest, solid, upstanding man. Well, until I ruined everything but that wasn't her fault. She'd never been given the opportunity to run me out of town. Which I'm sure she would've done as quickly as possible even before I got pregnant. We'd never met, and for good reason. I was trash, worthy of nothing more than to be tossed aside like yesterday's lunch.

Still, a parent like Bruce's mother was what I wanted for my child. One who would pour into this child only blessings. Never the hurtful things like I'd seen in my own childhood. Who would protect her child at any cost. Not stand on the sidelines and allow her child to be beaten to a pulp.

Or so I assumed as I'd never had a conversation with the woman, only based on what I'd witnessed in Bruce.

I'd try to talk to my child about things to avoid in life. Silly, I'm sure. No way an unborn child could understand a word I was saying. But I wasn't going to have any chances later. This child would never call me 'Mother.' I'd come to accept my fate in life, that as much as I didn't want to, there weren't other avenues for me to walk down. But I hoped this baby of mine wouldn't repeat my many mistakes. Wouldn't wander down my very dark path. Wouldn't end up in the same deep, dark pit without any way out. Wouldn't end up with the same regrets or heaven forbid, even worse ones.

But most of all, to not end up giving up the most precious thing ever given in life. Love.

I also learned to knit. Not for me. But to create something I could give to this child. A little token for my child to have so that he or she would understand that I did care. That I did love this little bundle I was about to give to another woman. No matter what anyone said, in the end, my heart belonged to my baby.

I made a tiny lacy dress and cap, in mint green to be neutral. Each night, I would snuggle on my bed and work on that intricate pattern for a while before going to sleep. I'm not sure why it calmed me, but it did. To the point, if I didn't work on the project, I wasn't able to fall asleep.

When I had been there for a few weeks, I got a roommate - Janet. Her first night, unlike me who sobbed, she stormed. Defiant at being given the same lecture as I'd received upon my arrival at this place. She fumed and paced our small space. Her footfalls echoing, her words crescendoing, her anger palpable. She'd stomped in, thrown her case in the corner and didn't stop for several minutes.

"How dare they tell us what we will or will not do with our

children!" She spat out. "How dare they tell us we're immoral! How dare they tell us we're dirty! How dare they tell us we're unlovable!"

I watched for a while, allowing her to wear herself out some. Which didn't take long, her pregnancy bump seemed rather obvious to me. Even though she tried to hide it with a rather large, overflowing dress, same as everyone else here. However, there was no denying the state she'd gotten herself into. She might even be further along than I was, hard to tell for sure. When she sank to her bed, taking a few sips of water as she did, I saw my chance to fill her in on the lay of the land.

"They're nicer to you if you just go along with everything. Don't sass back, do your chores without complaining. You're even given larger portions at meals and the easier tasks and chores." I sighed, I'd come to learn this was a war I couldn't win. "They hold all the power here, not you. In a few weeks you'll have the baby and go back to your life like nothing ever happened. The sisters keep saying how simple the whole process is."

She wrinkled her nose in disgust as she tipped her head, slowly putting the glass of water back on the dresser. "You backed down, simple as that?"

"Not exactly, but I've come to understand there's no way out except to leave here without looking back." I rubbed my belly, knowing that while I might never speak of this little person again, I'd never forget my baby. This child was as much a part of me as I was of it.

A few weeks later, my time came. I found myself ushered into a small, white, sterile room. Containing not much more than a small bed with stirrups for my feet and a metal table filled with medical instruments. Cold, bright, and scary. A man in scrubs and two nuns bustled around doing everything and nothing. Yet no one assisted me after I was told to lay down on the bed. A difficult task given that I was half bent over from a contraction.

A sheet was raised and clipped to two poles, this hovered at about my waist to hide what the doctor was doing. Leaving me a view of nothing more than the white walls next to me and the white ceiling above me. Cramped, confined, confused.

Every once in a while, one of the nuns would move a bit closer to the sheet. Just enough so that I would have a quick peep at her face. All I would ever be told was to push, over and over again. The pain left me feeling torn in two, I labored on. Screaming until I became hoarse and having no one respond. Faint whispering around the room, nothing I could catch or understand. None of those words were directed at me, I wasn't anything more than the baby's host.

A cry, nothing more than a whimper really.

"Is the baby a boy or a girl? Can I hold her?" I called, to anyone and no one. Afterall, I had no part in this drama – the baby was all anyone cared about. After several minutes, I got my answer. The bundle, now howling as it was held tight in the arms of one of the nun's, was rushed out of the room. Without me even getting a peep at it.

Without anyone bothering to tell me what was going on, the doctor and remaining nun finished their job. Pushing, pulling, touching places on me I didn't even realize existed until right then. Everything hurt. Yet I didn't believe I could question what they were doing or if the sensations I was experiencing were normal.

Later, as Sister Ann pushed me back to my room in a wheelchair, I tried to ask again, "I want to hold my baby. Please, just for a minute. Can I?" Twisting as much as I could to try to gaze up at her, I grunted as I did so. Despite the agony it created in my abdomen, I shifted a bit more.

"Dear, it's best if you never see your child." Her stern voice floated down to me, her eyes staring straight ahead.

Biting my lip, willing myself not to cry. "Why? Can you at least tell me if it's a boy or a girl?"

"It's easier to forget what you never know." She snapped.

We'd reached my door, not another word spoken as I limped towards my bed with no help from her. As I tried to find a comfortable position on the bed, I pressed on my stomach. The loss so great, so real, so permanent. It's not easy to put something out of your mind because you haven't learned one little fact. It causes more questions, it leaves a bigger hole in your heart.

Was this child even healthy?

There wasn't ever going to be a way to end the river of tears now. So sure I was that the grief I'd come to experience would never end, I had a brief flash of finding a way to end my pain forever. I had nothing left to live for, there didn't appear to be any reason to continue to live in this kind of misery. Yet I didn't even have the strength or courage to do that.

I'd have to live with the knowledge of what I'd done.

About an hour later, Susan, one of the girls who happened to be working in the kitchen at the moment came to my room. "Hey, I was asked to bring you some cabbage leaves."

They were pressed in damp cloth. Confused, I looked at them then back up at her. "Why?"

"To put in your bra to stop the milk." Simple, direct, statement, like I should have already known this. "If all else fails, at least they will be soothing." She added.

The next morning, I began to pack my things. Despite being sore, weak and tired from having tossed and turned most of the night. Beyond ready to move on, forget this past year, forget Bruce, forget everything. Just like the sisters kept insisting that I should do once the baby had arrived.

Janet took one look at me stuffing what little I owned in my case and fled, as fast as she could waddle. She was due any day, so that wasn't very quickly. A moment later, I sensed a presence in the room.

"And where do you think you're going?" Sister Ann had planted herself in the middle of the tiny space.

"Don't know and don't care." Not bothering to stop or even slow down my task that I'd almost completed at this point.

"Not yet, young lady. We can move you to a room in another area, however, you need to repay us for the services we've provided you."

Even though her hands were tucked inside the wide sleeves of her habit, I felt as if she was wagging a finger at me. As if she was scolding a small child, not speaking to a woman who'd given birth the day before.

"Excuse me?" What did she think I was? A prisoner? A servant? She'd invited me here, lest anyone forget that. But long gone was the girl who'd have said anything in return. Long gone was the girl who'd stand up for herself. Long gone was the girl who'd believed she could control anything.

"Pick up your case." Her habit floated around her as she spun towards the door.

I did as I'd been told without saying another word.

Time blurred over the next few weeks. Nothing mattered as I worked to repay my debt to these Sisters for helping me in my hour of desperation. Watching other young women come bearing their burdens as I had done, knowing what lay before them. Knowing I alone remained my sole friend in this world, but I hadn't taken very good care of myself. The baby weight dropped off my small frame, I became not much more than a skeleton, unable to eat or sleep as I mourned. Ready to go back out into the world and pretend I'd never been a 'fallen' woman, never made a mistake, never had a child.

Never been in love.

CHAPTER 13

New Mexico – Present Day

"They never told you what your baby was? How is that even possible?" Tim sat at the edge of his seat, his hands pushing on the wooden arms as if he was ready to spring up at any second.

"From what I understand, not giving the birth Mother any information was standard practice. And would remain so for many years after I gave birth. I've heard these stories on the news about open adoptions. Everyone involved is practically friends. But back in my time, nothing, and I do mean nothing, was meant to be shared. Everyone believed it best for the baby that the child be handed over to the adoptive parents with a clean slate." My throat closed tight, the pain from over fifty years ago still so raw I might have given birth yesterday.

"That's cruel." He hung his head, his whole body shaking. "I'm so sorry you never had any idea until now, Donna."

I didn't quite know how to respond, this reaction felt too strong to be from our conversation alone. He had to be wrestling with that problem of his own. How hard it must have been for him to never be told about his own adoption until recently. To have been led to believe for so many years he was one person when, in fact, he was another.

Secrets, so many secrets in so many lives.

He raised his chin enough to snag a slight glimpse of me, "Did you really want to raise her?"

"Looking back on things now, I'm not sure. As it turns out, she remains my only child. A big part of me regrets never having the opportunity to be a Mother. Never being able to hold a baby in my arms. Never watching her grow, make mistakes, fall in love, have children of her own. I'll never have any of those things." I looked out at the trees again, their leaves quaking in the breeze. "Some other woman got all of those moments with my child instead."

Everything always looks different when you look back, so many things you see in a new light. However, in my life, one fact never changed, I had never had anyone to turn to for help. People always disappointed me or worse. Bruce failed me. Well, I didn't quite give him any other options. Those nuns destroyed me. My mother set me up for disaster. Harry tried to kill me. And too many others to name.

Okay, that wasn't quite true. There had been a few over the years who have shown me a tiny bit of kindness. Nikos, and the priest in Zaragoza. And there was one person in particular who for all intents and purposes saved my life, Pat.

But did those small things outweigh all of the horrors I'd suffered? Even after the space of all these years, I couldn't tell. To me, the worst times in my life still loomed large. Dominating my thoughts despite all my efforts to banish them. There were days I would find more joy than sadness, sure. But in the end, I remained an old woman, alone and isolated from almost everything.

Yet one thing in my life never changed, I was a Mother to no one. I'd been robbed of that chance. For years, at every child I'd see on the streets, my body would freeze and tense as I wondered if he or she was mine. My jealousy at their mothers so real, raw, I'd often walk away angry because I wanted to be that woman so badly. Understanding full well that no child would ever want me as a Mother in the end. I'm so flawed and damaged, rendering me completely unlovable. My broken heart would lose a new piece each time.

"Are you sure about that, Donna? Are you really not a Mother just because you had to give her away?" Tim's words cut me deep, all the way to my wounded heart. "She's reaching out now. She wants to meet you for the simple reason that you gave birth to her. That has to count for something."

I snapped my eyes back to him, watching carefully as he rose and took the few steps to me. Placing a soft hand on my shoulder, he gave me a gentle squeeze. Not saying another word, he waited for my response.

"But why would this daughter of mine want anything to do with me? You mentioned she needs to see me, to know someone who shares the same traits. All because I happened to be the one who carried her in my womb. But that can't be enough." I closed my eyes tight.

I'd let her be taken from me, handed over to strangers. I'd never even mentioned her very existence out loud until now. And I'd had this conversation today not because I'd somehow found the courage to face my demons. Rather it had been because my hand had been forced.

By her.

"Because you're her mother." He whispered, as if the answer was that simple.

"But I'm not worthy of that honor." My face wet yet again from my tears, my emotions a raging sea.

"Why?" His hand tightened on my upper arm, giving it a firm massage. His eyes drilling into me.

"Because I'm unlovable. No one wants to be around people like me." I repeated the mantra those Sisters had told me over and over. But did I still believe it after all these years?

"Ah, you're not that bad. A bit on the prickly side, I've run into a few cacti that might be less painful to interact with than you." He chuckled. "Your brother doesn't hate you, right? At least he talks to you sometimes. Or did he only call you to fill you in about your daughter calling from out of the blue?"

True, my relationship with my brother wasn't cold. To be more precise, Stan didn't have strong feelings about me one way or the other. Most likely because I hadn't told him very much about myself. Or where I'd been since we'd last seen each other on the night I broke his father's nose. I'm sure he'd learned more about me from the fact my child had dropped into the scene than anything I'd shared. "That's complicated."

"You like answers that aren't answers." He gave out a deep hearty laugh.

"You're too young to understand that life doesn't fit into neat boxes or follow a straight line." I shot him a cross-eyed look full of darts. Tired of the mocking, tired of the banter.

"Hey, lady, I got lied to my entire life." He cocked an eyebrow at me as he pointed a finger towards the cabin he shared with his mother. "And it's not like I have a Dad to look up to anymore."

Yup, he understood a fraction of messy situations and thorny life problems. He lived in a place where every step you took landed you in quicksand. Or ripped you to shreds. "But here's the thing, I didn't straighten up and fly right after I had my child. I went from that problem to another one refusing to allow anyone near me ever again."

"Still doesn't disqualify you from at least having a conversation with your child. If I do decide to try to meet my birth Mother, I'm going to hear her out. Why she couldn't keep me, who my father was, if he was or wasn't involved in the decision to place me for adoption. And I also want to find out how she felt when my parents refused to reach out as part of the open adoption agreement. She's a person too." His pain and anguish for his birth Mother all too real. "Let your daughter have a chance to spill out everything she needs to, good or bad. Whatever it is, it's obvious she can't bottle it up forever."

I held my body still for a moment, thinking about this. There was one piece of my story I wasn't sure I could or should share with anyone. And that year flashed into my mind before I could wish it away. But this time, I let the images play out. Not stuffing them back into the far reaches of my mind as I normally would have.

CHAPTER 14

Arizona – 1968 - 1969

I'm sure Harry preyed on me because he had a keen sense of my weaknesses. In those early days after I left the maternity home behind I'd been so vulnerable. When he first spotted me on the bus bench in Phoenix, I'm sure he'd been delighted. He'd found a girl he could use as his new toy before tormenting her later. He could sense my loneliness, feebleness, pain, grief. Everything about me which made me an easy mark for manipulation.

I'd been doing my level best to not cry for days but had failed utterly and completely. I'd wandered the country on various buses that late October. Escaping the deep wrenching ache inside me wasn't possible. Leaving myself behind wasn't possible either, I had to live with what I'd done. I had no plan, in truth, no place to go. Yet, my gut told me I had to get as far from what I'd given up as possible. This world wasn't filled with sunshine anymore. What I believed about love and happiness had been snuffed out forever. I couldn't figure out what hurt more. Never holding my child, ever finding out if it was a boy or a girl. Or the knowledge that Bruce had failed me in the end because he'd never come back to rescue us.

Not like he had any clue where to find me.

My guilt and shame were written all over my face, as they had been for months. No longer was I the confident young woman who could wrap anyone around her finger. I'd become the fallen woman that everyone told me I was. I slunk around, my head lowered. My long hair covering my face, looking down at the floor. Never interacting with anyone unless there wasn't another option. I'd completed my tasks at the home and fled, to nowhere.

The leper who'd become an outcast trying to stay in the shadows.

I wore a heavy, dark brown dress, a chunky black sweater, both dug out of the 'free' box at the maternity home I'd just left. I now was unadorned with jewelry of any kind, no more baubles in my ears or beads around my neck. My hands bunched and unbunched the stiff, coarse fabric of the skirt. Over and over again as I sat. Alternating between staring at the dirty gray speckled laminate flooring and the schedule board, I ignored everything else. Knowing I couldn't remain there forever, my stomach heaved every time I glanced up. Seattle? New York? San Francisco? Tallahassee? The names blurred as my eyes misted over, nothing mattered anymore.

"Mind if I sit?" A voice chirped out at me, forcing me to crawl out of myself for a moment and notice the world around me.

A man stood next to me, tall and willowy. Leather fringe jacket, paisley shirt, jeans with flower patches, flip flops for shoes. His light brown hair hung in long greasy strands. The odor of patchouli and marijuana oozed out of every pore.

When I didn't reply, he slid next to me on the bench, taking my hand in his as he, with great care, stroked each of my fingers. "What's got ya down, doll?" He purred, brushing my cheek softly.

My body stiffened, I jerked away from his touch. Reaching out to grab my small case, I shifted away from this man as if he was the diseased one rather than me.

"Ah, no, girl. I don't mean no harm. Chill. We's good. I just hate seeing a gal cry, is all." He gave me a goofy grin, as he put his hands up in a surrender motion. "You go on to wherever, and get happy. Alright?" He slipped a few inches down the bench, cool as a cucumber.

At these words, I melted into a puddle of blubbering sobs as he engulfed me in his arms. Yup, I was putty in his hands. And in less than five minutes, I had agreed to leave the station and go home with him. Against my better judgment and all while I choked down the bile rising in my throat. Something about this whole scene wasn't quite right.

He was too good to be true. Because he, in fact, was the dangerous version of me even if I couldn't quite see that yet.

As we left the station, the blast of heat that is Phoenix almost any time of the year hit me. The warm sun felt good this late in the year after being up north. I'd witnessed the snow again for the first time in many years a few days before I'd fled. This place might be alright for me, a nice change of pace, a way to melt my frozen heart. My head rationalized that I'd stay with this guy for a night or two, and then figure something else out. Everything would work out in the end.

But I am me, nothing is ever right with the world.

Harry had been at the station to drop a friend off, or so he claimed on the long ride to where he lived. His dark blue VW bug wasn't new, but it had been taken care of. The seats had been covered with fuzzy blue material. The car polished and the dents had been repainted with flowers. It eased my mind a bit that he opened the car door for me, he took my elbow, in short, he acted like a gentleman.

At first, but that didn't last more than a hot minute.

He opened the door to his apartment with a flourish, waving his hand to usher me inside. "The bedroom's in back. Donna, you help yourself, I'll flop on the couch until you can find a better place to crash. Okay?" He brushed my shoulder, sliding his hand down my back stopping a few inches short of my butt.

"Thanks." Holding my case with care, I scanned the small space as I moved toward the bedroom.

Open floor plan with tiny combined living room/kitchenette. Single bathroom right before the lone bedroom. Bare furnishings which looked like they had all been tossed aside by someone else. Brown suede couch with denim patches. Single wooden chair with different colored legs near a metal table that leaned slightly. Chipped mugs on the counter. It wouldn't be possible for me to stay here long without cramping Harry's style.

Marijuana shabby.

The bedroom held a large bed, piled with unmade rumpled brown and white striped sheets. A patchwork quilt thrown on top that might've been a hundred years old, it was so worn. Plus a small dinged and scratched dresser stood in the corner, missing two drawers. The place reeked of incense. I tried to open the miniscule window beside the bed, but it turned out to be painted shut. I shuffled down the hall to the tiny bathroom. And found a shower, sink, toilet all in olive green with wads of towels on every surface. No window here and the scent of his musk made me gag. I did my business quickly before making my way back to the living room.

Harry danced around the kitchenette area, using a hotplate to cook on. "Hungry?" he called over his shoulder.

I nodded as I drew near, unsure if I should sit or offer to help.

"Chill. It'll be done in a jiff." He pointed his chin towards the lone chair.

I sank into the chair, steadying myself as it wobbled, gazing at him while he worked. Typical bachelor meal, mac and cheese from a box. He placed a plate in front of me and the table rocked as he did. The second plate he set across from me. Then he opened a closet door, grabbed a folding chair and sat so close to me our knees touched.

He shoveled food into his mouth so quickly that half of it fell back out onto the plate, "Where ya from?" the words muffled from his chewing.

I shrugged, "Nowhere really." Taking a small bite, I realized he's at least added some canned tuna to the stuff to make it a bit more filling.

He prattled on about his job at the university. A janitor, not anything important or time-consuming. According to him at least. Not appearing to mind at all I'd given him a non-answer.

When we'd finished, I offered to wash up, he waved me off and I wandered off to bed. I didn't hear him leave in the morning, but I found myself alone for the whole day. He'd left a note in the kitchen area, 'Help yourself!' I found a book of poetry and spent the day on the couch reading. Not eating much of anything, not wishing to have to repay him for any more than I had to.

He arrived home with a bag of groceries in one hand, "Hey, fix us something, will ya?"

As I rose, he shoved the bag my way. Not feeling the need to respond, I placed the bag on the few inches of counter space. I began to dig around to figure out what to make. I whipped up a simple hamburger dish, proud that I'd remembered something from when I used to make meals as a kid. Also glad he hadn't bought much. The small fridge wouldn't hold more than a half gallon of milk and a couple of pieces of vegetables. The thing stood in one corner, proud and pink with a pull handle. While it had a small freezer compartment inside, I doubt Harry had ever defrosted it. There wasn't any way to put something in there because it'd become so encrusted with ice. As I finished prepping our meal, I put the few remaining items away. Most went into the lone cupboard under the countertop.

Harry leaned over to kiss me as I started to sit after placing the plates on the table. I didn't want to go down the road of being with a man again. I knew where it led, even when you were careful. So much for the rhythm method. But he'd been so nice, what was the harm in a little smooch? I turned my head enough so his lips landed on my cheek.

"Not ready yet?" He whispered in my ear, "Maybe tomorrow." Then squeezed my thigh hard, leaving his hand on there for a touch too long.

I should have gotten up and ran. It shouldn't have mattered that I had nowhere else to go. My gut screamed so loud at me that something wasn't right with this situation. Yet, the fact remained, my purse had less than a hundred bucks in it. I'd been floating through life. Landing on this person's couch. Or that person's spare bed. Or in this person's van for far too long. I'd given up any semblance of safe and secure, no, I'd never had that to begin with.

No anchor in life for me, not once in my entire miserable life.

"I just left a bad scene, nothing against you." I lied as I pried his fingers off my leg.

"Gotcha, babe." He grasped my chin, looked at me with hard, cold eyes and gave me a long, hard, deep kiss. Finishing by biting my lips hard enough to leave me licking the acid tang of blood off them as I swallowed hard.

Stunned by his show of force, I didn't bother to fight or resist in any way. My body went numb as I accepted my fate. For Harry, my wishes were nothing more than dandelion fluff floating away in the wind.

And things went downhill from there.

It started with these little comments and jabs. Nothing I hadn't heard before, or that I considered unusual per se. But enough that I should've been aware that I wasn't in a safe place. Enough that I should've seen what was to come. Enough that I should've realized I needed to take care of myself first. But instead, I didn't do anything but float.

Because I didn't understand my own value.

"I don't like that dress, find a better one." He declared, as he ripped my dark brown dress off me. Leaving me standing there in my underwear with my torn garment rumpled at my feet.

I'd been making breakfast, unsure what to do next and didn't wish to have anything else destroyed either. "Uhm, okay. What's your favorite color?" I turned to him, trying my best to smile. Pretend everything was fine. That it's normal for your partner to ruin your clothes if they hate them.

All the while my mother's words about 'broken bones being the price you pay' were ringing in my ears. A ripped dress wasn't that bad compared to what she must've been going through to have made a comment like that. This I could handle, I could soften Harry's edges and make him love me. Make him less cruel. Make him kind and gentle, same as he'd appeared to be on that first day at the bus station.

I could make him perfect.

"Purple." He slapped my backside hard as he leaned in to nibble on my neck. "And show some skin."

The color I didn't have a problem with, but looking sexy I did. However, given the situation, I wasn't about to argue. Because, right then, to me, playing nice would allow me to move on with my day. Anything else might end up with me receiving another slap or worse.

After he left for the day, I got dressed for the second time and found a thrift store. Scouring for something, anything I believed he might like but that wouldn't be overly slutty. Not sure I succeded, but he didn't complain about the dress as we had dinner that evening.

A few days later, I mentioned something about talking to one of the other girls in the building. I'd been doing our laundry, nothing but a friendly chit-chat. His response? "You don't need friends, I'm all you need." As he jerked on my arm hard, pulling me into a tight hug.

I didn't think making a fuss about this comment would help the situation. Plus the pain he'd inflicted had been rather minor. But I decided not to mention what I did while he was gone again, not wanting to push my luck. I'm not sure if his reaction had scared me or just made me uncomfortable, or a mixture of both. In any case, I didn't wish to see anything like that again.

About a week later, I spotted a help wanted sign in the window of the cafe near the grocery store I typically shopped at. And the idea crossed my mind that it would be perfect for several reasons. If I were to ever leave Phoenix or Harry for that matter, I had to bankroll such a move. While I wasn't about to repeat my prior bad acts and be overly flirty with patrons, I thought I could still make a few bucks.

At dinner that night, "Harry, I'm going to get a job as a waitress again. Then I can pay part of the bills around here." Thought it best to share part of anything I'd earn, I'd been riding his gravy train for long enough. I'd stroked his arm as I said this. Trying to be a bit coy, making a few of my old moves, to show him who I believed to be the most important person in the room.

"You don't need to work, I can take care of you babe." He yanked on my hair hard, forcing my head back as he leaned over the table. Pushing the plates aside, he started to undo the buttons on my red dress. The second one I'd purchased after I'd discovered he'd tossed out most of my clothes. "Who paid for this new dress? What ya think? I'm not a real man?"

"No. Forget it." I murmured as I allowed him to do whatever he wished with me, as I always did. Even though I didn't like it one bit as we ended up on the floor, him writhing on top of me. I lay still as a stone, as I tended to with him. He'd hurt me otherwise, I'd learned that rather quickly.

A few days later, I rushed home, later than I'd expected. Not that I thought it would be much of a problem. I still would have plenty of time to whip up some dinner and have it on the table for him from what I could tell.

Harry stood beside the door, arms crossed over his chest standing guard like a sentry. "You weren't here when I got home. Where'd ya go? Who were you with?" He barked out as I waltzed in.

"No one, I got caught up reading at the library." I tossed my purse on the sofa, flipping my hair as I strode towards the kitchenette corner. Unsure why he'd gotten home early, not really caring in the end.

"I'm jealous, I like you all to myself." He followed me, tugging on my arm, spinning me around. "Just be home when I am, okay?"

I nodded, unsure why he'd gotten so upset over something so trivial. His grip got tighter, then he pulled me into the bedroom, I stumbled along, tripping to keep up. He proceeded to undress me forcefully, my desire to be intimate never mattered to him. I tolerated him having his way with me as usual, so much easier than the alternative. I hated him screaming at me, I hated him grasping me hard, I hated the hard looks he'd give.

Submissive had to be the way to go.

When he finished, he remained on the bed naked and sweaty. I rose, dressed and went to make our dinner. Ignoring the red marks on my forearm, again. They weren't a big deal, a small price to pay for free room and board. My mother had it worse, didn't she?

And life went on as I continued to pretend I lived with a prince not an ogre.

"This place is a pigsty! What do you do all day?" He screamed early one evening as he entered, pulling off his shirt and tossing it aside. He then proceeded to kick off his shoes, leaving them in his wake.

The house stayed clean until his arrival each evening. He tramped in all manner of gunk, so much so, I began to doubt his story of being a janitor. Not to mention the fact he'd claimed to only work a few hours and days of the week. Yet he always managed to be gone from early in the morning til dinnertime, seven days a week. Yet I never mentioned these discrepancies to him, my safer option seemed to be staying quiet.

Instead, I grabbed the broom and began to tidy up, same as I did each time he came home. "No worries," I muttered, trying to remain small. Exactly as I had when I was a child and Charles got angry.

Spring arrived, my birthday with it. I put on my best dress, the purple one he loved so much. I fixed myself up all pretty with my long hair up in a bun, makeup and all. Then, I perched myself on the edge of the couch and waited for hours. But Harry never came home that night.

I didn't want to shed a tear, but I'd tried hard to do everything he'd wanted and asked of me. I'd tried not to complain, not even about the put downs or the bruises. I lived in this little bubble as he wanted me to, no friends, no job. Nothing but him.

And he'd promised me this one little thing.

When he finally arrived, at almost midnight, he took one glimpse at me. All curled up on the couch still in my outfit, and burst out laughing.

"What got into you?"

"It's my birthday and you said we'd go out to dinner to celebrate." It would've been our first real date. The first time we'd gone anywhere outside of this apartment together in all the months I'd been here.

"Oh, I never said anything like that. You's crazy." He continued to chortle, deep from his belly, bent over as he slapped his thigh. "I had that thing with the guys. Ya know." And he strode off to our bedroom, reeking of beer and marijuana.

I wasn't an afterthought, I didn't even enter his mind one little bit.

And some little part of me screamed *"It's time to leave, get the hell out of dodge. Save yourself*! Well, my gut had been telling me that all along. But now I'd been slapped in the face with the reality that I meant nothing to Harry. I was there to please him, as a matter of convenience for him. He'd gotten a live-in maid, with the side benefit of sex whenever he pleased. Because I just rolled over and let him do anything to me.

I followed him towards the back of the apartment, burning with anger. I grabbed my suitcase from the closet as I entered the bedroom. Without a word, I began to pack the few things I'd brought into this relationship that still remained. Which wasn't much, he'd destroyed or thrown away most of my things. But I wanted nothing from him, he could have those things I'd purchased with his money.

"What's ya doing?" He'd already flopped onto the bed, in his birthday suit as usual, revealing every inch of his very white skin. Because he always wanted one thing from me, nothing more. Not tonight, not ever again.

"What ya think?" I snapped back, not looking at him.

"You're just lucky I found you that day at the bus station, Donna. And you know it. I'm the best thing that's ever happened to you. You'll never find anyone better because you're from the gutter. Ha, you'd have to work up to that." He leapt from the bed and threw my case back into the closet, half packed with clothes and all as he laughed snidely. "You're a whore. Always have been, always will be."

Discussion over.

There was no coming back from that remark for me. His arrow hit the bullseye and what little resolve I had dissolved in a flash. As I lay in bed that night after we'd been intimate, my pillow became wet from my silent sobs. I felt those heavy chains from his comments holding me here. The walls in that small room came closer to me. The tiny window became smaller, making my prison even harder to leave.

And the leash got shorter, until it choked me.

I'm sure the blame for this could be placed at my feet, at least a large part of it. Because I would never speak a word in my own defense, never stand up for myself and say that very simple word 'no'. Not once. Still so wounded, the words of the nuns echoing in my ears, 'No man will ever want you now.' Harry wanted me for his own twisted reasons, I didn't deserve anything more. He'd been correct in his assessment that I'd hit the jackpot landing in this pit of despair.

There wasn't any place better in the world for me.

And by staying silent, did I imply I'd given consent to Harry? Did I send him a signal that I didn't mind the put downs, the insults? Did I, in fact, give him the green light to do whatever he wanted to me no matter how much pain that might inflict? Except for that one night of defiance, I never fought, never showed an ounce of resistance. No, I remained passive, still, accepting. Thus, those little hurts and pains he inflicted were but warning signs.

Because the worst was yet to come.

The harsh words he flung at me fueled his anger and now a few things were thrown, or smashed to accentuate his points. Those little bites and nibbles became flesh tearing, those hard squeezes became punches. It never mattered if I tried to be meek, use calm words, or apologize for something I hadn't actually done. He'd explode anyway.

"It doesn't take that long to do one errand." His words cold as ice slapped me without warning one afternoon as I entered our apartment.

I'd come in from the grocery store, my arms laden with bags. All to end up ducking the glass thrown at my head as I opened the door. Why he'd come home early I didn't have a clue, my churning gut warned me it wouldn't be smart to argue. Again.

"Sorry," I murmured as I bent to retrieve the items I'd dropped among the shards. Pricking a finger, I noticed a drop of blood expand on the brown paper bag. And wondered for a second how this had become my life. But there remained only one reason for this, I'd followed my mother down a very dark path. Dropping that thought as quick as it'd appeared, I pretended the world around was still normal. Smile. All's good. "I'll make your favorite for dinner, babe."

His anger escalated to a few extra slaps, then a few harder punches over the next several weeks. I took each one as stoically as possible. Always they were in places I could cover up the bruises left behind with a long sleeve blouse or a turtleneck. Thus I could continue to delude myself into believing that all was right in the world. And never show those marks to anyone outside of our home.

At first.

When he switched from punching my sides to my face, I had no choice. I had to hide at home for days until the swelling subsided. When those few questions did come, I'd make some excuse. Like I'd been sleepwalking and hit the doorframe or some other bit of nonsense.

"I don't like cold food. I warned you when I'd be back." He'd stormed in two hours late, slamming the door in his wake.

He'd marched right over to the counter where I had his dinner waiting, covered with foil. He'd snatched up his plate, sending it sailing across the small apartment. Bits of food flying off leaving a trail of debris in its wake. The dish itself didn't shatter because I'd switched to Melmac after all the others had been destroyed. Instead it bounced off the wall and clattered to the floor.

I wondered for a second if my mother was still playing the same game of replacing dishes and glasses every other day. All because Charles did the same thing Harry did - smash everything in sight.

"Sor…" I began before his hand reached out and forced my mouth shut. His grip so tight, the pain shot up towards my forehead.

"Sorry don't cut it, babe." His lips curled into a snarl, as he shook my head around. "Where were you all day? Be careful, I'm the jealous type and I'll kill you if so much as look at another guy." His hand released me only to swing back and hit me so hard my ears were ringing. "I was here earlier and you weren't, so don't lie now."

I couldn't even wrap my head around the threat he'd made or what to do next. I'd been there all day and Harry hadn't come anywhere near the apartment. I couldn't figure out what he was talking about. But to contradict him might lead to another punch, to tell a lie might as well.

"Laundry." The middle ground might be safe, I lowered my eyes to the floor.

"Bitch." And he swung a few more punches before dragging me off to our bed.

Why he needed to make love after being so violent I didn't understand in the least. But this had become his pattern lately, giving me a good thumping before forcing himself on me. The swing of it left me cold, my body wouldn't respond. Resulting in me hating being in bed with Harry, hating him touching me in any way at all.

I felt dirtier with him than I did with all of those men I slept with before Bruce.

And I began to tiptoe around everything from morning to night. Afraid of each sound. Afraid of making one false move. Afraid of being me. There didn't appear to be any way to predict what would set Harry off. Today it might be the wrong thing for dinner. Tomorrow it might be him imagining something I did or didn't do. The next day it might be something I was wearing.

In the end it didn't matter much what I did, his rage continued to build and my injuries continued to become worse.

A few months later, I was sitting in a hospital room, getting stitches in my face, arms and legs. My head swimming, my eyesight blurry. My ribs aching. My throat sore and each time I swallowed, I swear, shards of glass were going down, it was that excruciating.

As far as I could tell, my life was over.

That day, his flash of anger started over something in the mail. I'd stopped picking it up after he'd flown into a fit one day about me reading his private stuff. Didn't matter to me, not like any of it was addressed to me anyhow. Thus, I'd conceded the point, even if I'd never opened one single piece in all of those months. I'd been careful to place it on the table in a neat stack, untouched, pristine.

"Hey, what's this bill for?" He called as he walked into the apartment, flipping the piece of paper against the envelope it'd come in.

"Don't know, what's it say?" I'd been cutting up a few veggies for dinner, now twisting my neck towards him, unsure where this was going. I never spent any money other than the few bucks in cash he doled out for the household allowance.

"Bitch, you're stealing my money!" He grabbed a mason jar I'd found at the thrift store that I'd been drinking out of. It was half full of water, as he snatched it off the table and he threw it my way.

I ducked as it whizzed by my head, the cool water splashing over me as it continued on its path. It ended up hitting the wall behind me, shattering into a million pieces. He continued to smash coffee mugs, throw plates. Moved on to the knick-knacks I'd picked up here and there to make the place more 'homey.' Whatever he found handy he hurled towards me. I sank onto the floor, curling into a ball, knowing what would come next – me. In the end this day would be the last, his rage the worst I'd ever seen.

As his booted feet began to slam into my sides, I tried to crawl under the table. But he grabbed me by my hair and banged out a rhythm on the linoleum floor with my head. The whole world became wavy, I no longer cared about Harry or what he thought of me.

I only wanted the agony to end.

What seemed like only a moment later, Harry had straightened up and moved a bit closer to the wall by the couch. He'd put several holes in it as he punched and kicked it rather than me. Confused for a second, I realized I'd passed out for at least a minute. Taking the opportunity given me, I tried to slide towards the door without making a sound. The broken remains of everything in the apartment scraped every inch of me at each little move I made.

"Oh no you don't!" He screamed. Grabbing my feet to pull me back to him, then my arms as he jerked me up to stand beside him. "Where's my money?! You don't leave here until I get it!"

Nothing about this made any sense to me, and I didn't see a way out. "Don't know..."

"Argh!" He grunted as his strong arm wrapped around my throat like a snake, spinning me around. Pinning me tight with my back against his chest, locked in an embrace as he squeezed tighter and tighter. Trying to wriggle free, I kicked, I pulled at that arm, nothing worked. My breathing became raspy, my stomach heaved, every part of me tingling. His arm loosened for just a second as he adjusted his grip. On pure instinct, I bit him.

Not my best move, I'm sure.

However, that is how I finally got away. This startled him enough, he backed off for a moment. And it was precious time that allowed me to run to the open door. I flew down the hall, into the stairwell, and finally into the lobby of the apartment building. I could see the end of this nightmare. I spotted the light streaming through the window of the front door of the building.

The two police standing beside that door had other ideas.

As I pondered this in the hospital, a small part of me understood the terrifying ordeal might be over. I'd escaped. How luck had played into me still being alive, small little things working in my favor. The rest of me wished Harry had finished the job. Because I might still be in danger.

"Miss, did you hear me?" The policeman asked again as he stood beside my hospital bed.

Yes, I'd heard him. From the moment I'd been ushered into the police car to be taken here to the hospital he'd been saying the same thing. The person in trouble was me. Somehow, me taking a chunk out of Harry's arm was a crime. Yet, Harry beating the tar out of me wasn't. I gave a small nod. Flashes of jail went through my mind, being labeled a criminal on top of being a whore. And I'd thought I couldn't sink any lower.

"Sir, I need you to leave for a few moments. We need to fully examine the patient and we can't do that with you in the room." The doctor waved towards the door, his feet firmly planted as he stared down the officer.

"Fine. I'll be right outside, so you can't go anywhere, Ma'am." He growled as he stomped into the hall.

The nurse patted my hand, "They brought your purse with you, don't suppose you have anything else of value?"

I shook my head 'no.'

"We will admit you for a few days, by then the police should stop hassling you. Then you can just walk away. You need to find the strength to go as far from here as you can." The doctor looked at me with a slight grimace, kindness in his eyes. "I wish we could do more for you than patch you up and send you on your way. But you have to help yourself, get out, leave this man. Next time, I doubt you'll end up here. Mostly likely you'll end up in the morgue."

"One of us nurses will find you a few items of clothing, dear." The nurse stroked my hand. It felt so soothing despite the enormous amount of achiness and discomfort I now battled.

I blinked hard, this gesture of compassion from strangers I found hard to accept. People in my world aren't helpful. I switched my gaze from one to the other, looking for some reason to doubt this offer, to not trust them at this moment. I twisted my lip, gnawing on it for a moment, unsure of everything.

I nodded my head 'yes.'

There had to be more to this life than pain, sadness, sorrow. I needed to find a place that brought me joy, peace.

CHAPTER 15

New Mexico – Present Day

A ll of these memories from my brief time with Harry flashed through my mind. However, Timothy shouldn't ever be told any of it. I'd always believed some things were better left unsaid, hidden, buried deep. It'd made me uneasy over the years when I'd heard other women share their stories of abuse. Others calling them 'brave,' 'courageous,' 'warriors.' How they could stand up to the monsters who wounded them so deeply, I never quite understood. Yet, there must be power in shining a light into those dark crevices.

And maybe, just maybe, if I shared my story it would help someone else not fall into the same traps.

However, I remained quiet. Allowing what Harry had done to lurk in the dark recesses of my mind and heart. Had he done something similar to anyone before me? Or after? Based on what I'd experienced, I could guess that answer to be 'yes.' But I wasn't the one to stand up and slay the giant that was Harry. I did hope some woman with a lot more courage had.

To this day, I don't know who alerted the police to our fight, if one could even call it that. I'm also unsure if things are better now, or if women still receive the third degree as I did from the officers. Harry had followed me in my rush down the stairs. And upon seeing the policemen had loudly proclaimed I'd attacked him. Nothing I said after that mattered. They kept telling me I shouldn't have defended myself. I shouldn't have touched Harry. Never should've bitten him. I guess to them I deserved every lick I got at the hands of my abuser.

End of story.

"I'm not going to fill you in on the ugly details, but suffice it to say giving up my child destroyed me. I landed in such a deep pit I almost allowed someone to kill me. Despite all of the warning signs, I didn't leave a very bad scene. Then a few kind strangers reached in and pulled me out." I rubbed a knuckle against my jawline where a slight scar still remained. Wondering if saying even that was giving too much away.

"I get ya." He stood up, pacing the small porch. "We all react to grief differently."

Grief.

That summed up everything in a nutshell. An overwhelming ache filled every inch of me back then. Not just the physical pain from so many bad experiences but emotional wounds as well. And I couldn't see a life without it, not for a very long time. Even with the help offered to me after Harry, it wasn't easy to move on to something better. In many ways, I never did recover from those injuries. I let Timothy continue his stroll as his thoughts gelled, wondering where he would land.

"When my dad died, I got mixed up in the wrong crowd. Part of the reason Mom wants me so close now. But, at the time, they made me feel something, anything. Before I started hanging with them, everything was numb, raw. Not sure how to explain it." He stopped, wrapping an arm around a post as he looked out over the mountains. "But they exploited me, used me for their gain." He spun towards me again. "Now I've got a record and my great future has a giant blemish on it."

Which explains why he was bored and ended up digging through boxes in an attic.

"Find a hobby. I know that sounds silly, but it'll help. Trust me." I stood up, "Give me a second."

I marched into my cabin, straight back to the far corner of my bedroom. To the spot that held my prized possession, a small token but the thing I held most dear. Returning to the porch, I placed the object in Timothy's outstretched palm.

He twisted the rock over and over in his hands, observing every tiny crevice of its two or so inches. Every bit of it painted with tiny, intricate pink and white roses. My first major piece of art and the sole piece of mine I'd kept over the years.

"My little hobby." I gave a slight snicker, a massive understatement given what my art was worth in certain circles.

"You made this?" He sucked in his cheeks, letting out a low whistle. "It's amazing!"

I beamed as I lowered myself back onto the swing. "As I learned to heal, body and mind, I created that and many similar items."

With great care, he placed my talisman back in my open palm, "How?"

"Ah, that was my Sedona year." I wrapped my fingers around my rock firmly. This tiny anchor, all that remained as a tie to a beautiful soul who'd given me more than she would ever know. "Someone guided me to finding things buried deep inside me that I didn't have any idea were there. Good things, lovely things, things worth saving among the rubble."

He bit a thumbnail, pensive and unsure. "I don't think anything in me is like that. Good I mean, not the art part."

Because he didn't have the benefit of age and a bit of wisdom yet, he didn't see his full worth. Not like I had much more knowledge than he did, but I at least understood he'd landed in a very deep rut and needed a boost out. Not sure that his mom would approve of me trying to push him to move on with his life. Leave the proverbial nest. Go find his true value and stand as a man out in the great big universe. Yet, it did seem that someone had to.

"Uhm, while it's not my place to say this, but I know you're wrong. What lights you up? What brings you joy? Let's start there and see if we can find that one thing you can do. The thing that will move you into the point of fulfillment and contentment. You might not be able to make a career out of it like I have. However, it might allow you to see the world a little differently." I tapped on the arm of the swing with my fingertips, trying to think of something else encouraging to say. Human connections weren't my strong suit.

He gave out a dry chortle, "You sound like you could be somebody's Mom. Great advice there." He shoved off the post he'd been leaning against and sank back into the chair.

I wasn't sure if he was mocking me or praising me. "Are you going to take it?" I wagged a finger at him, ugh, such a Mom move there.

"Not sure. I play guitar some, don't think I'm good enough to perform or anything." He did a few air guitar motions with a flourish. "Don't do more than strum a bit in my room, where no one can hear me."

I beamed, an excellent place to start. "YouTube can help. There's lots of videos to learn to play various types of music and techniques to improve your skill level." I may not have a great grasp on the internet, but that website I'd scoured for years. All kinds of useful and weird information to be had there. "What's your favorite - rock, classical, Spanish?"

His hands stilled midair, frozen over his pretend guitar. "Ya think? I mean, professionals are on a whole other level." He gulped, "I love playing ballads, that's kinda old school but they speak to me."

"How did my painting techniques progress? By spending hours every day with a pencil or brush in my hand, creating something. Not everything turned out like I'd hoped or planned. And that was okay, sometimes even better. Just keep at it, you never know where it might lead." Not wishing to give him false hope, I decided to throw in something to lower his expectations. "If all else fails, you'll become good enough to give lessons."

He went back to picking and strumming, pondering my words. Silence washed over the porch for a few minutes as I watched him. His long fingers were perfect for reaching the far chords. For elegantly stroking the stings. He'd been genetically designed for this. For a second I could hear the melody he might be playing. Almost asked him to run home to grab his guitar, but that would've ruined the moment.

His mother wouldn't have let him come back, she'd force him to go back to his chores and not keep dilly-dallying all day.

He gazed back over at me after a while, "Who taught you to paint that rock?" He nodded his head towards my hand. "Let's face it, you're too old to have used the internet to learn that. Those brush strokes are so fine, dainty. I can't imagine how you did that without smudging everything."

"Thanks for throwing my age in my face." I let out a small chuckle, not offended in the least. "And the trick is to use the right materials. One of the sweetest women I've ever had the pleasure to meet introduced me to art. She also taught me some of my most valuable lessons on life. " And time spent with her was one of the things I missed most in life.

CHAPTER 16

Sedona – 1969 - 1970

In the end, charges against me were never formalized and the police never did come back to the hospital. I didn't ask any questions about what had happened with that. I also thought it best not to poke the bear, a.k.a. Harry. Thus, I stuck with my original statement that nothing I owned was important. Clothing and my few other bits and bobs were replaceable. I didn't have any desire to go back to that apartment ever again for anything.

A nurse arranged for me to stay with her aunt until I had healed, at least a little. I'd ended up so stiff walking more than a few steps wasn't possible without excruciating pain. Those nurses pampered me, taking such great care as they moved me in and out of my bed. Washing my long hair to remove the blood, then making sure it was kept brushed so as not to become knotted. Finding me several items of clothing so I'd leave the place in something other than a hospital gown. Their kindness at times smothering, hard for me to accept. Because I didn't' deserve it, hadn't earned it, understood why I'd landed in this mess in the first place.

Still, I didn't fill these nice, upstanding women in on my past.

That last afternoon, I'd been wheeled down to the lobby after spending more than a few days in the hospital. My body bruised from head to toe, too many stitches to count, broken ribs, concussion, black eye, the works. Boxers came out of the ring looking better than I did. Wearing a soft pink dress with huge white flowers all over it. A pair of sandals on my feet that were a tad bit big. Clutching my purse like it was my sole anchor left.

She stood there in the middle of the room waiting for us. An older woman sporting gray hair pulled back into a sloppy braid draped over her shoulder. Wearing a bright multicolored tie-dyed t-shirt pulled into a knot at her side. A long blue flower print skirt swishing against the floor. Plus a giant grin on her round face.

She held her hand out as soon as she spotted us approaching, "Hi, I'm Patricia, but just call me Pat!" Leaning over slightly to make it easier for me to accept her gesture.

"Hi," I mumbled, my head lowered. My hand pulling my blonde hair forward like a curtain to try to hide the stitches on my jawline just below my ear.

She reached over, with gentle fingers raising my chin. "Never hide who you are dear. Scars, warts and all. You are beautiful, always remember that."

I stared deep into her dark brown eyes, trying to figure her out, to tell if she might be lying to me. Because I honestly couldn't remember anyone ever telling me I was beautiful before. Not even Bruce. I wasn't that kind of girl. The kind you say nice things to. The kind you take home to meet your mother. The kind you marry.

No, I was the kind you used, abused, and tossed aside like yesterday's trash.

Her thumb slowly began to wipe the tears off my cheeks, careful to avoid the damaged parts. "We'll fix this and everything else, dear." She nodded to the nurse, her niece, "Thanks honey, we've got this. I'll call you soon and fill you in on how everything's going."

A moment later, I lounged in her car, propped with comfy pillows for what turned out to be a several hour drive. In the back of my mind,

I'd believed this person lived in Phoenix. And I'd been dreading the thought I might run into Harry at some point. Mostly because I had no idea where he worked, there was more than one university in this town after all. And that most likely had been a lie to begin with. And I hadn't really learned anything else about his life either. I'd asked so few questions in the year or so we were together. I'd allowed him to dictate everything, which wasn't good.

As we wove along the highway, my mood shifted. Each mile not only moving me one step further from my problems, but one closer to the solutions. As if by magic, I could sense the weights being taken off my shoulders one by one. To the point, for the first time since I'd entered the hospital I fell into a deep sleep.

I'd been having attacks of sheer panic, every little noise had made my heart race, as dread filled me. I'd become so certain that Harry had returned to finish the job of killing me, each second more fearful than the last. Oh, and those moments where a shadow crossed my door and every inch of me would tense. Because, again, my first thought would always be *'It's Harry.'* Catching my breath had been impossible, not for the broken ribs alone.

Every moment had become a nightmare that I couldn't wake from.

A soft voice wafted into my dreams, "Dear, please wake up. We're here. I'm aware you need sleep and lots of it, but you'll be much more comfortable in your bed."

Shifting a bit, I opened my eyes, one still so swollen it couldn't see more than a fraction of what it should. Pat's warm face greeted me, she reached over to squeeze my hand with such a light pressure I almost couldn't sense it. Then she brushed a loose strand of hair off my face, staring right at my stitches.

I grunted in pain as I sat up straighter, holding my bruised side. "Sorry."

She shrugged, "For what? Being human? I heard all about what happened, my niece made sure to fill me in. And this isn't my first rodeo,

I and several others have helped women who've landed in the same mess you did. But don't get me started on that. Let's just say, there needs to be some better laws and a safe place for women to go. Or for men to act less like apes." She snorted as she hopped out of the car.

I started to follow but opening the door turned out to be more of a challenge than I was capable of at that moment. However, she came to my aid in an instant. She helped me out of the car with great care, then held my elbow as she guided me into her home.

The quick peep at the exterior I got was something to behold. She'd filled the sandy yard with bronze sculptures of all kinds of animals, both mythical and real. Dragons to lizards, trolls to children, unicorns to horses and everything in between. All had been artfully displayed in and around various large cacti. The main home itself a simple log cabin, melding into the rocks of the canyon wall behind it. We took the few steps up a flagstone walk to the steps leading to a large front porch. It'd been filled with various chairs each with an easel set before it.

"I teach art." Pat didn't believe any other explanation necessary. She opened the oversized door with the massive brass handle shaped like a horse head.

The large space, warm, cozy. Calm infused every inch. She'd used soft rust and turquoise colors for the furniture, accent rugs and pillows. Couches and chairs in one section, a modest kitchen with a large table beyond. The exposed logs served as beams holding the cathedral ceiling up. Chandeliers made from antlers hung in various spots around the space. The pine floor worn with the pattern of years of footfalls. They'd turned an almost white hue compared to the darker tan of the log walls.

"There are artists in residence at times, right now, none. Thus, you can have your pick of the bedrooms." She turned and began to go down a long hallway lined with artwork. Numerous doorways exited off the hall, all filled with bright light from the rooms beyond.

I could taste the salt from my tears as my tongue wet my lips, "Why?"

Without looking back at me, her heart told her my question had nothing to do with bedrooms. "Because you deserve more than you will ever comprehend."

My sobs could no longer be contained, my screams echoed down the hall. Sinking to my knees, she caught me as I did and cradled me until my torrent had been spent. This was the beginning of my healing journey, when I faced what I'd tried to ignore for weeks, months, years. When I allowed all of my stuffed pain to come out in a flood. No words needed to be spoken, but I'd come to the point of being fully broken and undone.

Nothing in my life had ever been okay.

Over the next several weeks, I began to heal. My progress slow, painful. I began with short hikes on the path in the canyon behind the house. A few feet at first, stopping to rest by finding a boulder to sit on. Gazing up at the stripes in the rocks, wondering at the pressure and the years it took for those to form. Listening to the birds sing and call out to each other. Hearing the quiet stream whisper to me as the water flowed over its bed. Observing the deer come to drink, their timid moves as they did, not wanting to be caught out in the open.

I found a small measure of peace I'd never known before by being still, alone.

At night, my dreams became less haunted. My bouts of panic lessened, my sense of unease weakened. No, these things never went away, simply became a manageable part of my existence. They didn't quite control me, yet I didn't seem to control them either. A sudden loud noise still made me jump, but I no longer burst into tears or curled into a ball.

This had become the new me.

Pat gave me the space to find me. She seldom spoke to me except at mealtimes. There was an understanding that what I most required was something no one could give to me. I had to do this work on my own. Yet her kind and gentle spirit spoke volumes, just being in her calm world was enough. She watched me like a hawk, without interceding.

There was one thing that Pat did do for me, she gave me a small sketchbook for me to take as I wandered. I tried to mimic what I noticed, putting everything around me down on the blank pages. However, my first attempts were ugly, crude, distorted.

Rather than getting frustrated, I understood what this proved. Again. How fundamentally flawed I was. How impossible it was for me to do anything right. But since art was Pat's whole world, I continued. I wanted to make her happy, to repay her in some small way for her generosity. But none of my work came out any better, no matter how hard I tried.

One night at dinner, Pat reached over and clasped my hand, "How's the drawing coming?"

Gulping, I didn't want to admit to her it'd proven to be yet another one of my failures in life. "Uhm..."

"After we finish, show me. We'll be able to see where you need a bit of coaching, no one starts out as a Michaelangelo." She chuckled, squeezing just a bit more.

Nodding, I wondered who this Michael guy was and why she wished to compare me to him. But I didn't want to appear stupid in her eyes, so I didn't ask the obvious question.

We washed, dried, and put away the dishes together as we always did after each meal. A simple task we did in tandem, silent, side by side. We had this rhythm down. She'd do a dish, pass it to me. And I'd give it a quick wipe with the towel before placing it on the shelf beside me. Most nights I enjoyed the task, comfortable, mindless, relaxing. I'd take peeps out the kitchen window. I'd often spot deer wandering into the back garden for a nibble at the lettuce. Or a bird perched on the fence railing. Once a skunk slinking towards the shed.

However tonight wasn't the same, normal, right. My stomach twisted in knots. A large part of me hoping she'd forgotten about my sketchbook by that point. I fumbled with each plate, almost dropping a few. I couldn't look at her, resulting in the whole exercise being out of sync. I started to make a move towards my bedroom when we were finished. Hoping beyond hope this night would just be over if I disappeared.

But no such luck about Pat forgetting her desire to view my sketchbook. As soon as we were done, she nestled into her favorite large cushioned chair in the living room. Pulling the lamp on the side table a bit closer to her as she did.

"Okay, let's take a look at your work." She gave me a warm smile, her eyes lit up with excitement as she clapped her hands.

I didn't want to disappoint her, art being her whole world, but my attempts wouldn't ever measure up.

I bit my lower lip and without a word, finished the trip to my room to retrieve the stupid book. Wishing for all the world I'd ripped the pages out and tossed them away in the trash. Or better yet let them float away in the stream to melt into nothing in the water. Returning, I stood in front of her. With trembling fingers I held out the small, thin book. Most of the pages filled at this point with, in my opinion, very bad art.

She opened the first page with great care, studying it and turning the page slightly. Since she took so much time with that first image, I figured this would take a while. I half stumbled to the other side of the room to one of the other chairs. Sinking down, I continued to watch her as she flipped to the second page. Her face filled with wonder and excitement. Not the reaction I'd expected.

I twisted my hands in my lap, unsure what I should be doing. *Did she really like what she saw? But why?* Or did she view my work the same as she always had seen me? She didn't focus on the obvious, instead, she fixated on what lay beneath. The beauty she believed to be hidden beneath the pain, the scars, the flaws.

Something like a half-hour later, Pat closed the sketchbook, tapping it with her finger. "I'm surprised at how much progress you made in such a short time. You've been here, what? About six weeks now? And look at how far you've come." She paused, taking in a deep breath. "Donna, how much art history have you learned?"

Well, that was easy. "None." As I released some of my pent-up tension.

"I see real potential in your work. As of tomorrow, you're one of my students." She rose and came to me, handing me my book with great care. "Treasure this, your early work will always keep you humble."

She opened a whole new world for me, in more ways than one.

Never sharp or critical, but always willing to show me how to be better, to do better, to grow and learn. Art became so much more than doodles on a page for me, it became an obsession. I'd find little objects on my hikes and bring them home to paint on. Unusual rocks, bits of wood, rusted cans. I needed to turn the unwanted, the unloved, those things that were tossed aside into something beautiful.

Because then, and only then, could I believe I could be too.

Pat used some herbal salve on my healing scars, leaving little visible. But the ones in my heart, soul, and mind couldn't be removed so easily. I remained jumpy for months, anything being dropped sending me right back to that last day with Harry. So many nights I found sleep wouldn't come. Thoughts coming unbidden, replaying everything from that relationship. Counting out how many things I might've done differently even before I'd met him. Figuring out how many regrets in life I already had and I wasn't even twenty.

My pillow seldom would be dry in the morning, my weeping uncontrollable.

Every once in a while, Pat would put my things in her gallery to sell alongside her other students' work. She invited me to visit, to see my work on display. Yet, I wasn't ready to leave her property, or the silent canyon in the back. I seldom even interacted with the other students who came for lessons. Preferring instead to remain to myself. People were dangerous.

And I wasn't any better at knowing how to deal with anyone. I hadn't learned anything no matter how many times I'd gotten burned. I always came back for another licking, or two, or twenty. No, I'd be better off alone, isolated. It wasn't like I continued to blame myself for what Harry had done to me. I'd slowly learned to shift that onto him and him alone. But I did have a deep sense of shame at myself, hating myself that I hadn't been strong enough to help myself.

And just walk away the first time Harry hurt me.

One morning at breakfast, Pat reached over the table to hold my hand hard and firm. "Sweety, it's time."

I blinked hard and fast. My stomach clenched tight, I closed my mouth as firm as I could, willing myself not to cry. She'd had enough of me. Thoughts raced through my mind of what I'd do now. I didn't have a dime to my name. When I'd first gotten here and dug through my purse, all my money was missing. Not sure who'd taken it out, but my guess had been Harry. Nodding, I gave the only acceptable response, "Okay."

Knowing nothing I said would change my fate.

"You've outgrown me and what I can teach you. I bought you a ticket to Paris. I'm going to give you some traveler's checks, more than enough to have a good start. From there, you'll have to find your own way. But the most important thing, you need to go study the masters. Go to the Louvre, Vatican, Athens, Vienna, wherever. Find every church, cathedral, museum, old building you can. Immerse yourself in art. You get me?" Her eyes welled up with tears, she tried to smile but failed. "I love you so much, honey. But you need to dig deep within yourself, find that inner beauty you're hiding. Then put that on a canvas for the whole world to see. The world needs to see your passion, your heart, your soul. Put that into your work, make it speak for you. Tear down those walls you've built."

CHAPTER 17

New Mexico – Present Day

V ery few were aware of the humble beginnings of the artist I now was. Even fewer had ever heard my real name, as I always signed my pieces with only my initials, DJ, and a symbol of a dove. My work hung in galleries all over the world, yet I'd never stepped foot in any of them as an artist. Yes, I'd been in many of them. As an unassuming visitor there to admire the pieces along with the other nameless faces in the crowd. I didn't do the gallery openings expected of artists, not my scene. I also didn't do interviews, never had my photo in a magazine.

I was and always would be a shadow.

As my mind wandered back to those few months with Pat, I wished now I'd kept that sketchbook as she'd suggested. But I'd been so free back then, so aimless, the weight of possession more than I could bear. Thus, my small rock alone had survived, buried deep in a pocket of my backpack. I didn't take it out often, it was enough to know it was there.

Timothy chuckled, "I figured you were mailing some kind of artwork because of the shape and size of the packages. Can I see your work, beyond this rock that is?"

I grimaced, pondering this request. While on the face of it, this question appeared to be simple, straightforward, benign. However, to me, it was the equivalent of letting someone see me naked. And no one had done that since Harry. The seeing me in my birthday suit part, not the viewing my paintings part. I didn't want to be that vulnerable, exposed ever again. There had been some level of safety in keeping others at arm's length. At not letting anyone be close enough to understand anything about my life. To never showing more than this false front I presented in public.

My work needed to stay anonymous.

Yet, as my pause to give an answer drug on, I noticed that Timothy's face changed. A not so subtle shift from being excited to looking for all the world like I'd just slapped him. And somehow, I didn't want to hurt him by refusing his request. Still I hesitated. So many pieces in my home were unfinished, flawed, not quite ready for public consumption. However, this fragile bond we'd begun to build now had begun to crumble. All because of my unwillingness to be open, vulnerable about something so simple. How could I say no?

Besides, he already had learned most of my secrets.

"Sorry, I shouldn't have asked." He turned his face from me. "Guess I should be leaving now, I read ya loud and clear. I've overstayed my welcome."

Scratching my eyebrow for a second, I knew the right thing to do here. Rising, I coughed to get his attention and motioned for him to follow. My heart fluttering, my eyes twitching, my hands shaking as I opened the door to my sanctuary. This space was mine and mine alone.

Until now.

I'd turned the living room into my studio, which was the reason I'd requested to clean the small cabin myself. To avoid prying eyes, not because I was some kind of clean freak who had to do everything themselves. My easel stood next to the far window, various works in progress strewn around the room. Paints, brushes, boards, jars of water, and the other tools of my trade rested in weird places. The furniture I'd pushed into a corner. Allowing me the space to pace. Or adjust the easel when I needed a different angle from the light. Or wanted a slightly different view of the world around me.

Timothy strolled around the small space, gazing at each canvas. He repeated his amble around everything. This time stopping to squat down for a better view of several that were resting against the wall. The third time, he stopped and crouched before a piece that caught his eye. One that might have been about two-thirds of the way finished. Sunset on the mountains. Vibrant golds and reds of the autumn leaves, with a lone cactus standing guard over the valley.

"This one is my favorite. You've managed to make this look like a photo rather than a painting, How in the world did you manage to do that? I can see every spike on the cactus! Rather cool." His finger hovered just above the canvas. It followed various brush strokes along the form of the cactus, waving in midair.

Beaming, it surprised me at how warm inside I became at his praise, so much better coming from him than anyone else. "It's nothing special, I learned to copy the masters just like Pat told me to do. Several famous artists do a similar technique, not overly difficult once you get the hang of it."

He stood. Wobbling a bit in an awkward movement from being in a bent position for so long, "Thanks for changing your mind and showing me all of this." His arm swept the room. His face aglow with astonishment at being allowed to view an art gallery exhibit privately.

"No problem, again, they're just my modest attempts at making a few landscapes. Yes, I sell a painting here and there, no big deal." No need to have anyone try to compare me to Picasso or Rembrandt, or anyone else along those lines. My work wasn't ever going to end up in the Louvre or the Prado, I'm fully aware of my place in this world. Didn't matter what any of those art critics said. And some of them had given me glowing reviews over the years.

He squinted at me, skepticism written all over him. He held my work in a much higher place than I did, and a pang of regret washed over me for agreeing to show him my work. I didn't need approval, to be given a pat on the back. Then I stopped myself from going down that road again, reminding myself that I'm worth something. My gift has merit and should be admired.

I'm not the broken woman I was in my twenties.

"How long were you in Europe?" He shifted to stare at a different piece, one with a cactus in full bloom at sunrise.

"Most of my life." I swallowed hard.

Maybe I should've stayed there, my life there had been easier, safer. If I'd never reconnected with Stan, then I wouldn't be wrestling with this particular problem right now. What am I supposed to do about a child I'd had nothing to do with in over fifty years? But something happened about five years ago which forced me to face the fact I needed to find my mother. Which had led me to my half-brother instead. Come to think of it, several conversations had tried to show me the importance of family.

"I've been here my whole life." He shook his head, sad puppy dog eyes. "Never been anywhere else."

I took him by the elbow leading him back outside. Pointing towards the mountains, "Which is perfectly okay, you have all of this beauty all around every day. Let's take a walk and I'll tell you all about my adventures." Slipping on my hiking sandals, I grabbed my water bottle. I always kept both beside the door for easy access. Then with brisk strides, I went down my steps and around the side of my cabin to the spout to fill it. My favorite path which led to a small stream took off from there and that is where my feet wanted to go.

A moment later, he caught up to me and hooked his arm in mine. "Tell me everything."

CHAPTER 18

Europe – 1970 - 1990's

Getting to Europe turned out to be easier said than done. A few hectic weeks were spent obtaining a passport for me. Picking out a few clothing items and essentials that would fit into my new backpack. Teaching me a few basic phrases in French and Italian. Pat assured me I'd find other American kids my age wandering Europe. There to try to run away from the political problems in America and the Vietnam war.

My whole generation felt the need to escape something.

But she didn't need to tell me to stay away from those hippies and deserters. I'd left that life in my wake already and had no desire to return. Calm suited me. And while I hadn't quite found inner peace, I sensed I'd found a path that might lead me there.

In the early morning hours, we sat in her car for a moment in the airport parking lot in Phoenix. Our last few seconds together, my heart breaking as I realized what I was losing – a Mother. She'd loved me unconditionally from that first second in the hospital. She'd given me more kindness than anyone ever had. However, I didn't fully understand or appreciate these gifts she'd given me until now.

And now I had to move on, fly out of the nest like a good baby bird should.

"Sweetie, this will always be your home. Not just because it's the place we've listed as your address for those pesky government forms." She leaned over, wrapping me in a warm hug. "Whenever you need a place to sleep, you're welcome. Donna, go be great."

My voice cracked as I managed to squeak out, "Thank you." However, those words would never be enough to repay her for all she'd done for me.

Our embrace might have gone on all day, neither of us wanting to let go. Yet I had a plane to catch, a new life to go find. She pushed me softly away, holding me out to have a good look at me. "Go make me proud. Get your work in the most famous museums someday." She gave me a twisted smile, the best she could do, her pain at losing me written all over her face.

Stumbling out of the car, I wrestled the large pack out of the back seat of the station wagon. Sliding one strap on my left shoulder, I started a slow stride toward the bright lights of the terminal. As I neared the door, a magnet tugged at me. I gazed back for a moment, at Pat standing beside her station wagon with the wooden paneled sides. One arm wrapped in the gauzy white fabric of her top draped over the open door. Her bright red and pink peasant skirt flapping around her. For all the world she looked broken, beaten by the weight of some terrible burden. Hesitating for a heartbeat, I debated about running to her. Yet, somehow, I understood that would hurt her more.

She had given everything to me, more than she could've afforded to give. And not in terms of money.

My first airplane ride should've been exciting, fun, thrilling. Instead, my thoughts were consumed with Pat and the fear that I'd made a mistake. Again. By the time the flight landed in New York, I'd managed to work myself up into rather a tizzy. At that point, I'd made up my mind to figure out a way to find a flight back to Phoenix. From there, I'd hitch-hike the many miles to Sedona. Then find a way to scrounge up enough dough to repay Pat for the cost of this little fiasco.

Scanning around the area, I couldn't figure out where to go to retrieve my backpack. Stumped, I figured I'd have to ask someone about that when I asked how to switch my flight. One more bit of proof that I didn't belong here. I didn't have the first clue about the rules of travel. Heck, I didn't even know what had happened to my stuff after the nice lady had taken it when I checked in.

"Nervous flier? Or first-timer?" A deep voice broke into my frantic thoughts.

Whirling around towards the sound, hoping beyond hope the man might be an employee. My heart sank when I spotted his dark gray, slightly rumpled suit and wide blue tie. Nope, yet another business man like so many had been on my first flight.

"Uhm," I wasn't sure where to begin or even if I should dump all of my problems into this guy's lap.

He took me by the elbow, guiding me to a hard plastic seat.

"Well, let's start with the basics. Is this your final destination?" His kind smile made the corner of his eyes crinkle. There was a slight streak of gray in his brown hair, deep lines in his olive skin. Thus, I pegged him to be much older than I'd initially thought.

"No, Paris, to study the masters. As in art. But I think I need to go back instead." I blurted out, he seemed safe enough.

"Young lady, I don't think it's as simple as saying 'I want to go home,' to switch flights." He gave a small chuckle, not mocking but as if he understood what was really going on in my head. "But I doubt you've been the first person to get cold feet on a flight. As luck would have it, I'm going to Paris as well. Pan Am at 6 PM?"

I nodded.

"Come with me, we'll eat a bite of late lunch while we wait. And you can tell me what's in Paris that you don't want to find after all." He gave another small laugh.

For reasons I couldn't explain, most of my fears and doubts melted away with him. As we chatted for those few hours until we needed to board our flight, he prattled on. I found out all about his family. How he was born in France and still had a few relatives there. Even though he'd immigrated to the United States as a small child. We practiced a few additional phases that he thought I needed to add to those I already had learned. He also told me about a few places he believed were not to be missed in his native land.

"Art can't be housed in the great museums alone, my dear. We hide it in every nook and cranny in every city and town. It's in the buildings, it's in the streets, it's in the walls, it's in the farmer's fields. Keep your eyes and heart open." He gave me a wink and a wise nod.

Paris in the early seventies wasn't for the faint of heart. Tourism hadn't quite touched and changed it yet. Thus, it still remained a city where men wore berets and sported small mustaches. They roamed the city on their bicycles, weaving in and around the narrow streets. Women hung their laundry out to dry together in courtyards. All while they chatted with their neighbors on the next balcony.

And outsiders were viewed with a touch of suspicion.

Yet, France, as a whole, was in the midst of social revolution. The modern world had begun to creep in, leaving chaos in its wake. I learned snippets about this. How students had changed the course of their country shortly before I arrived. The demonstrations, the marches, the riots. The youth wanted fewer rules, to be allowed to determine their own fate. My French language skills not good enough to understand all of what I'd heard. My new flat mates English nonexistent for the most part. But I understood that the world around me was shifting, moving. Evolving into something new.

Even if I wasn't.

I'd stayed at a small hotel for about a week upon my arrival, making inquiries about a place to rent. My limited amount of travelers' checks wouldn't last long. Well, not based on the price of that rather dingy, cheap hotel. I didn't need much, but it had to be at a rock-bottom rate. One of the maids at the hotel overheard me ask the clerk one morning about how to find a place and pulled me aside.

"I have room." She wrinkled her nose, searching for the right words. "Girls, tree." She held up three fingers to ensure I'd understood her.

"You share an apartment with three people?" I tried to help her by filling in the missing words.

"With you. Come, I show." She tugged on my arm. "I Belle."

"Hey, I'm Donna. Thanks." I gave her a goofy grin as I matched my stride with hers.

We walked several blocks, to a large cream and brown building with maybe five or six stories. She pulled open the heavy wooden front door and double time marched up several flights of stairs. Pulling a key out of her uniform pocket, she opened a small blue door. My eyes drifted to the other doors on a landing, each had been painted a different color - red, purple, yellow, green.

As we entered, Belle shrugged her shoulders, pouting her lips. "Nice, no?"

The large living room held two oversized pink couches with fat cream pillows. Off to one side, a small area held a counter with a hot plate and an assortment of coffee cups, and a small sink. There were two cream straight-back chairs with a small table beyond. Nestled next to an open window leading out to a tiny balcony beyond.

"You like?" She grinned at me. She walked down a small hallway. The first entryway had a curtain hung over it, partially open revealing a tiny bathroom. Odd little room with a toilet and shower, no sink. Four other doors led off somewhere, she opened one pushing me inside. "For you, yes?"

Small ironwork framed bed touching three of the four walls. A four drawer dresser that I couldn't see a way to pull the drawers open more than an inch or two. A window looking out towards the brick wall of the next building. A corner with a sink weirdly stuck in it with enough room to stand there as long as the door was closed.

Perfect.

"Yes," I answered, satisfied with this rather basic closet of an accommodation.

During those first six months in Paris, I focused on studying art. Paintings, sculptures, anything with a bit of beauty that caught my eye. Art needs no words, it speaks for itself. I found a job washing dishes at a small café around the corner from the flat I shared with those three other young women. Why that café? Easy, I'd discovered a few British expats frequented the place. It became somewhere I could speak freely with someone and be understood.

My roommates I chose not to become close to. Not because of the language barrier. Rather, to me, the safer path appeared to be the one of keeping people at arm's length. I'd breeze through the common living room, giving a wave and a bit of a smile. And make a beeline to my room where I'd hide out until I believed everyone else had fallen asleep. Once I figured out everyone's schedules, I went so far as to shift my timing. Thus, my comings and goings were almost unnoticeable. The walls to protect my heart were high and I kept adding a few bricks to them each day.

My life became busy, chaotic, safe.

A few months later, I used most of my savings to mail a few of my newest pieces back to Pat. Unsure what she would think of those paintings I'd been working on during that time. I couldn't figure out which of the artists I'd seen in the museums to copy. Or if I should create my own style. I'd ended up with a rather eclectic mix of works, all leaning toward the darker side.

I'd slipped in a letter, a cheery bit of fluff to appease her. Ensuring her that I hadn't fallen off a cliff and to fill her in on where I'd ended up living. Most of it was half-truths, the rest out-and-out lies.

Her letter back held an answer, of sorts.

Dear Donna,

I'm happy to hear you've found a few friends along the way. That may be more important than the artwork.

I will put the pieces in the gallery, however, I feel these are merely one more step in a very long journey for you. Maybe try Italy? Or Greece? Or just some of the smaller towns in France?

All my love,
Pat

My heart sank at these words. I'd failed her. These girls I shared a flat with couldn't be called 'friends' by any stretch of the imagination. I hated myself for lying to Pat. I dreaded the fact I'd been trying to make her think I wasn't wasting this gift she'd given me. And that my work reflected all of that. I vowed to do better.

Not for me, but for her.

And I began to wander Europe, seeing the social upheaval that was the seventies first hand. So many countries with problems. Demonstrations, unrest, people unhappy with the world around them. Which I understood, even agreed with on some level. But I always moved on before I got into any real danger. Never allowing myself to become pulled into the drama of the moment. France, Italy, Greece. Didn't matter where I went, the world spun out of control.

Still art had to remain my focus, not politics.

The world changed around me, yet I remained unchanged in so many ways. My heart unable to move past that moment in time when I'd given birth to a child I'd never know. My body unwilling to move past that day Harry almost beat me to death. My taste in food didn't change, my clothing neither. I acquired new possessions only to replace those which were no longer usable. I drifted as an observer not a participant in life.

Frozen, I remained frozen as a teen, never aging inwardly.

But my paintings and drawings were another story. My work grew, developed, took on a life of its own. I'd seen writeups calling my pieces heart-wrenching, soulful, painful. My grief spilled out no matter what I worked on. Fields of flowers in full bloom would end up being dark, brooding even. Beach scenes would end up being done on a stormy day, foreboding, ominous, heavy clouds being the focus.

However, they sold and sold well.

One evening at the end of December the late 90s, I lounged on the outside patio of a café in Athens. The large heater kept the chill at bay, yet I alone had chosen to not be inside with the handful of others. Not like many were out on such a dismal evening. It had rained heavily earlier in the day, now the sky had cleared as the sun had set. Leaving the temperature to plummet and everyone scurrying for somewhere warm. Most tourists were elsewhere this close to Christmas. Places with snow for skiing. Warm beaches for sunbathing. Or markets with Christmas themes for purchasing presents. Athens having none of those things hadn't been anyone's destination. Leaving it almost deserted, untouched.

My type of place to go.

My dinner half eaten, my massive sketchbook in hand as I gazed up at the Acropolis. The full moon beamed down on the many columns. Helping to illuminate the many shapes and lines of the centuries-old building. Something magical hung over the hill, a sense of wonder. And this had been my reason for picking this particular place to dine that evening. The great unobstructed observation point.

I'd never seen this place in this way before in all of my visits.

I'd tried to capture my vision with the hope of turning it into a series of paintings later. My hand now still as I'd ended my last stroke, waiting to see if there were any last-second details I wished to add. I sensed a presence behind me, staring at what I had drawn.

"You show dead." Deep voice, with a thick accent. "No correct."

I wasn't sure if he was referring to the fact his sentence wasn't right or if what I'd put on the page wasn't accurate. Either way, I didn't think I needed to respond. I don't listen to critics, my work would remain mine. If people didn't like it, they could go find a piece they did.

Beauty truly is in the eye of the beholder.

He shifted his weight, moving to the other side of the table. He slid a chair off to the side a bit so as to not hinder my view before sitting. "Your gift special." He pointed to an outline of a shadow, then did a quick look up at the hill as if seeing the sight before him for the first time. I'm sure, for him, the Acropolis had become something normal, everyday. Something he didn't even bother to notice most of the time, because it remained there, no matter what.

"Thanks." I took a good look at him. His large frame held tight muscles under his jeans and white polo shirt. His white hair still had a few streaks of gray along his temple. His mustache and beard both more gray than anything. His square face, tan and lined with wrinkles, his large round glasses low on his pulpy nose.

"You no like food?" He waved towards my plate, giving me a slight frown.

"Oh, it was wonderful. Just got pulled into the sketch, didn't want to lose the light from the moon. I'll finish every last bite, I'm sure." Giving him a quick smile, I wondered why he cared.

"Good, good. I wish customer happy. I own café." His face beamed with pride as he tilted his head up towards the sign above us, 'Nikoc,' in bright red neon. He snapped his fingers over his head, a second later a waiter came outside. He said something in Greek that I didn't understand, spoken too fast and low for me to quite catch. "I Nikos."

I took a quick bite of the now cold spanakopita, savoring the tang of the tzatziki sauce I dipped my potatoes in. The waiter returned with a platter of something and two glasses.

"You try. Dolmades and ouzo." He slid one glass my way and the plate he left halfway between us.

I picked up the green leafy-filled bite, popping it into my mouth. Not wanting to offend my host, I didn't mention I knew exactly what they were. I'd been in Greece off and on over the years, I wasn't a tourist. He'd heard my words and believed what he wanted to. Stupid American who came to Europe on a whim and would return home with a few stories. Never to return.

But, the last time I'd been in America had been for Pat's funeral in 1989. Cancer. I'd flown in and out of Arizona in less than three days. My skin crawling with dread at losing the last string I had to this world. That nurse, her niece, who had put us together in the first place had offered to have me use her address as my new homebase. Knowing I had no other options, I'd accepted, and only because I learned she no longer lived in Phoenix. Yet, I'd never visited her, not once, since. A few long-distance calls, a few letters, sure. It remained a business arrangement, nothing more.

Nikos and I relaxed for a few moments, savoring the food, the liquor, and the sights before us.

"I from Mount Olympus, north. Family raise sheep. I need city, move here. My café only serve family sheep." He thumped his chest.

In the dim glow from the small white Christmas lights strung on the patio, I tried to get a better measure of this man. Someone filled with pride and love for a family he'd abandoned, yet somehow managed to remain so close to. His heart had called him to something greater than the humble, rural farm life. But then he'd turned around and helped ensure his family's future. I'd spoken to others over the years who, like me, had left their family in the dust and never looked back.

However, his man reminded me of Bruce.

A flash of aching longing filled me, I hadn't thought about Bruce in years. I tried to stuff those memories down, knowing the damage I'd done to him. How I might have broken his bond with his family. How I might have ruined his chance at a future. How he might have been killed in a war he shouldn't ever have been in. Where was he now if he had managed to survive?

There remained but one way to turn my mind onto something else.

Picking my sketchbook back up, "May I?" Waving my pencil towards him, and pointing to the page.

"Draw me?" He shrugged his shoulders, sitting up a bit straighter.

My hand began to form the outline of what I had in mind, this gentleman with the Acropolis behind him. "Tell me more." I needed him to be comfortable, he'd stiffened, become grim. This didn't fit the image in my mind, didn't work for what I wanted.

Nikos prattled on about his childhood. The reasons he didn't want to be around sheep anymore. How some day he wanted to see New York City. As he spoke, the lines on his face deepened, revealing the many years he'd lived more than his words.

"Why you hold deep sad?" I'd been half hearing him at this point, my focus on the lines and shapes I'd been forming, and I'd almost missed his question.

I blinked hard, freezing for a moment. My drawing felt complete, or close enough and I set it down. Slapping the cover closed as I did. "I'm happy." I mumbled as I took another sip of ouzo, the fire biting me all the way down my windpipe.

"No joy." He reached over for my book without asking for permission. And began flipping through earlier pages. "God give great gift. Your hand make world come life on page. But no honor God."

He pointed to a picture, then moved on to another one. Each one dark, melancholy, heavy with sadness, dripping with grief. The work I'd become famous for, the emotions I'd learn to live with, the way the world looked to me, colored in shades of gray. Finding shadows where there were none. Finding gloom in the brightness. Finding despair where there should've been pleasure. Pat had often commented on the fact my art would sell better if my themes were less gothic.

Yet I'd never changed, never got out of the rut I'd been in.

He came to the last, his image. "Different." His fingers gently hovered over the page. He raised his eyebrows searching for the right words to say in a language that wasn't his first. "Here love, joy, peace. Place same," He turned the page to my previous attempt at the monument before us, "no good here." He waved over the picture. "No God here."

To me, the answer appeared rather simple, and it had nothing to do with God. I didn't compose art based on subjects who were in a good place very often. Those who'd found a measure of contentment, who had achieved something with their lives. Those types of people I tended to avoid. The homeless encampments in France in the 70s, I'd done a series of paintings with those as my focus. The various refugees who'd arrived in Europe over the years, yup, I'd done those too. The angry guy screaming at nothing on a street corner, well, I did that a few weeks ago.

Yes, deep inside me so much more lay behind the darkness in my art. Misery sucked me in, I understood that better than anything else in this world.

But I could do a sketch differently. And, tonight, I'd been compelled to repay this man's kindness by giving him a portrait with a bit of hope, happiness. Thus, I'd done this bit of art with the intention of giving it to him. What was different wasn't my work, or me, it was my subject. However, how to explain this to him didn't seem to be as easy as that.

"I want you to have the page I drew of you." I reached over for my book.

"No." Taking great care, he pushed the pages together, sliding the tome back to me. "You make many pictures happy. Come back and give me." He patted my hand, nodding his head. "Make peace with God. He make you more great."

Lowering my head, I pushed a knuckle into my eye hard, willing myself not to cry. For reasons I couldn't fully comprehend, I wanted to make this man proud of me. For him to love my work. For him to walk into a gallery and see my paintings on the wall and say, 'wow!' More than anything else I wished I had been born into his family. To be part of something so wonderful as that. Because then I'd have been secure enough to have found a new place to land, grow and flourish at some point in my life.

Not be the drifter that I was.

I owned nothing in this world, no car, no house, no family. If I disappeared one day, no one would notice or care. I was a meaningless spec on this planet, with little merit or worth. Who really cared about all of the paintings I'd created? In the end, I'm sure the answer was no one. This man would forget me the moment I paid my bill and walked out of his cafe. I shouldn't be getting this upset over his words. Or a few brief flashes of kindness on his part.

However, the whole bit about God had me rattled for some reason. Yes, I'd spent more time in churches over the years than most believers. Yet not to worship, never to pray, never to seek guidance from some unknown being. Rather to soak in the art and architecture. I'd ignored those who were there to genuflect and pray to something I felt sure didn't exist. Always with a sketchbook at the ready, I'd sit for hours. Taking in every inch of the place from gilded ceiling to mosaic floor. To centuries-old tapestries on the walls to paintings on the columns. To statues in the niches to coffins resting on pedestals. Even the prayer books and hymnals could lean towards the artistic.

But could there be something out there? And could I have touched on something bigger than this world for a brief moment tonight?

"I'll try," I whispered, tilting my head towards him not completely sure what I'd agreed to. As he wrapped me in a warm bearhug, a warmth I'd never known filled me.

For Nikos I'd do almost anything.

CHAPTER 19

New Mexico – Present Day

"Is any of your earlier work still around?" Tim stopped right in front of me in the middle of the trail, bouncing in anticipation. "Because I'd love to see something 'gothic' or 'dark', that's how you put it, right?"

I coughed, doing a calf stretch for a moment to gather my thoughts and best decide how to respond. Those pieces weren't me anymore. Yes, I'd made them and had earned a decent living with them. But something had changed that night with Nikos. My black and gray world began to have shades of color. While I'd discovered a small sense of calm with Pat, after Nikos I found a few things which could bring me a touch of joy. If I let my heart be open to it. Joy comes from within, I had to be in that state.

But being in emotional harmony wasn't something I was good at.

"I believe several smaller museums and a few galleries have a few of those pieces, yes. I'm aware of several collectors who do. Many artists have darker works from periods in their lives that brought them pain, I'm not alone in this. I think depression is common in those who are on the artistic side." I shrugged it off, acted like it wasn't what it was.

I'd been grieving for nearly thirty years and for some reason, Nikos snapped me out of it. Maybe it had been nothing more than I needed someone to point out the obvious. Or maybe my grief had run its course and it wasn't anything more than a coincidence. Or it was possible, while I still didn't fully believe in God, I did now sense a presence when I sat in churches. Because Nikos had planted a notion in my head that He might be near. Might have a part to play in my life and in how Pat had saved it.

"Did you go back later and give Nikos your sketch?" He leaned against a tree, one leg bent as he put a foot up like a stork.

"Yes. Several years later I had a showing at a small gallery on one of the minor islands of Greece. I wanted to pop in not as the artist, but as a tourist to get a sense of the layout of the place. Anyway, I made a point to stop for a few days in Athens on my way there. Nikos and his café were right where I left him. I gave him a painting, one I considered one of my best plus the framed item of him from my first visit. I'd turned it into a formal portrait in oils but on the back of the frame I'd included the original pencil drawing." I cracked my knuckles, my face all smiles as I remembered that moment I walked in with my presents for Nikos. His great care as he'd taken the brown paper off both pieces.

"He was so delighted, he had one of the waiters hang both on the front wall beside the door right off. We had a fabulous lunch, staring up at the Acropolis of course. We write often, those letters from Greece you bring to me in the mail," I looked over at him.

Timothy's mouth opened then closed with surprise. His eyes growing wide.

"Yup, those are from Nikos. Hard to tell, I know, he puts his address in Greek, mine in English. Funny man." I chortled. "In case you wondered, I email him back. He feels the need to send me little things, I don't."

Timothy shifted his position and sank onto a large boulder. I could tell he was trying to do some mental math, trying to guess how old Nikos might be at this point. He tapped his fingertips, both hands indicating a rather large number. "Does he still run his café? Because, come on, he's got to be, what? One hundred?"

I laughed so hard at this, I snorted. "Oh goodness no, he's in his eighties!" Rubbing my eyes, I sobered a bit. "His son manages the café, Nikos has retired back to the family sheep farm. Where he's perfecting the art of making ouzo."

What I didn't feel the need to mention, how much of a hermit monk he'd become. Each time we'd met over the years, Nikos had become better at spouting scriptures at me. And more adept at applying them to my wayward life. After the death of his wife in late 2009, he'd gone home to his beloved mountains. Yes, officially he's taken up residence within the boundaries of the family's property. However, instead of moving into one of the main buildings, he'd built a shack for himself in the hills. To be alone with his grief as he'd put it in a letter he'd written to me at the time.

And my letters from him soon became filled with lessons for me about sorrow. About learning to live again after a great loss. And more along that vein. In each, he'd include a little pressed flower or blade of grass. In many ways, Nikos sensed while my paintings and sketches were brighter, my soul had remained heavy. There were still nights I cried myself to sleep, pondering what my child might be doing, where he or she had ended up. Unbidden thoughts about Harry or Bruce that I would stuff down as quickly as they'd pop up.

Basically, I'd been driving myself mad with what-ifs and what should've been for over fifty years.

Timothy's eyes clouded over. His mind drifted toward far-off places and things he struggled to imagine. After more than a few moments, he took a deep breath, "I'd love to meet Nikos sometime." A wish he shrugged off the moment the words escaped his lips. He looked to the ground as his shuffling feet kicked up a small cloud of dust.

I tipped my head, taking in the child before me. Had he been honest when he said he'd really never been much further than the town a few miles up the road? At his age, I'd been all over this country. Add another year or two, and I'd seen most of Europe. Was this normal? Not my life, his. Did kids these days never wander? Never go out in the great wide world and find themselves like my generation did?

I snapped my fingers, this was an easy fix. I never spent money on anything much. Goodness only knew what was going to happen to the sizable amount in my bank account when I finally kicked the bucket. "Well, let's go. I'll buy the tickets." This shouldn't be something that seemed so incredible, so out of reach for someone his age. "Guess you need to go apply for a passport."

He gulped hard, his Adam's apple fighting to stay in his throat. "What?!" He slapped his knee with an open palm, lifting his head back up to stare at a spot far beyond me. "What'll Mom do without me?"

"She's a grown woman. She'll figure it out." As much as I wanted to will this into being, my head and my heart screamed loud and clear. This was an impossible thing I'd proposed.

Timothy remained tied to his mother's apron strings. No, it was worse than that. He'd been wound up so tight in them he couldn't reach for the scissors. And this is why he struggled so much with his little problem today. Honestly, to be wrestling this much over having a conversation. To fill in his mom on what he'd learned about his adoption. That was rather insane to me. Yes, hello pot calling kettle black.

He looked down at his feet again, and changed the subject. "So, how'd you end up here? Kinda sounds like you had it super good in Europe."

"I blame that on Zaragoza." To be more precise, the priest at my favorite little church. I began to stroll along the narrow dirt path again, as more memories flooded my mind.

CHAPTER 20

Europe – 1990's - 2019

After my night in Athens with Nikos, I began to seek out what caused the shadows. Rather than the shadows themselves and what lay within them. My work shifted, evolved and took on a whole new meaning as I played with various sources of light. Trying to find what makes beauty, what brings hope, what brings joy. For me, this remained an elusive mystery much of the time. To find something worthy in the ashes of a broken world, to not see only the pain in the destruction man created.

I went back to many of my favorite places, to find a different perspective on what I'd believed to be true. As I stared up at the stained glass windows of saints in oh so many churches, I realized something important. When the churches were dim inside the light would shine through the brightest. Especially if the window was set to face the east or west. And I began to haunt sanctuaries of all types at sunrise or sunset just to witness this effect.

The light drew me in and began to thaw my cold, dormant heart.

There now were moments when I'd sense a presence next to me. Something I couldn't describe or even begin to understand. But this unseen thing would wrap me in warm, leaving me comfortable, at peace. At times I wanted to scream, *I don't know you, are you real? Are you always here? Do you care about me and my suffering? Do you love me? What are you?!* More to see if the answer echoing back at me from these sacred walls would be my voice or that of someone else.

I never did. Not sure if I was more afraid of what would happen or disturbing the quiet of these havens.

But I could now spot a family with small children and not weep, longing for what I could never have. I could now walk a little taller, smile at shop clerks, make small talk with people in the street. In short, appear to be a more normal person. Not a miserable old woman, sunk in the mire of despair.

At first, my new art pieces didn't sell. People didn't know what to make of my shift from dark to light themes, from brooding to hopeful. However, new markets opened up to me, new galleries picked up my pieces. And life continued on.

One morning in a small, ancient chapel in Zaragoza, Spain, I sketched furiously. My ear caught the faint whisper of cloth rustling as a person shifted in the aisle behind me. Ignoring this intrusion, I continued to focus on my subject. On the sunbeams filtering through the window. My pencil flew across the page as I tried to catch the fleeting moment I'd come for. When the face of the statue in the corner glowed as the light hit it just so. To most people, it would remain yet another Madona piece. She'd stood there, motionless for a hundred years or more, holding the Christ child. Battered, worn, dulled.

However, right at this moment, she became real. Her features now had a sense of movement to them because of the motes of dust. The ravages of time disappeared in the warm radiance, making her appear to be young and fresh. And best of all, her lips pursed just so, making it look like she might be singing to her child.

Pure magic.

The ancient wooden bench bounced ever so slightly as someone sat next to me, "You be here long time. I novice when I see you start."

I swiveled my head a smidge to take a good look at my intruder. And

I almost broke out into laughter. At the whole idea I'd been loitering here long enough for this man to age from youth to middle age. But my gut told me his words held more meaning beyond the obvious. Why had he been watching me over the years? Afterall most men are rather young when they start training for the priesthood, so for him to first spot me when he was but a novice must have been some time ago.

This simple priest in his black slacks and black button-down shirt with the white tab in the collar, now stood beside me. He hadn't ever spoken to me, until now. Not once in all of the times I'd visited this small church.

Not like most people bother to notice me or take a moment to have a conversation.

In life, I'm on the outside looking in. I often remained quiet, pencil and sketchbook at my side. And in places like churches, I absorbed the stillness and calm that they provide. Often not moving a muscle for hours. Not inviting others into my space. Not welcoming them to intrude on my personal introspections. A certain kind of peace could be found within these walls. Didn't matter if you happened to be in a church in France, Romania, Turkey or Spain. Did I believe in a higher being, in the God these buildings were for?

Unlikely. The presence I often noticed had to be something else entirely.

As I'd remained silent, he decided to fill in the gap, "Come." Motioning with his hand, then tugging on my sweater sleeve when I didn't budge.

Giving a small shrug, I picked up my things, shoving them into my small day pack. I shuffled out of the side door, following my guide, wondering what he wanted from me. He slipped through the side alley, ending up at a small coffee shop around the corner. He plopped down at one of the tiny outdoor tables, pulling out the other chair for me with a gesture.

"Speak here, better. I Father Antonio." He whispered something to the young woman who approached the table. "My English no is good. We try, yes?"

Sure, we'll try to have a conversation. I'd been bitten by the curiosity bug and it wasn't like I had anything better to do. He'd ruined the precious second I had that morning to capture what I'd come for. That would have to wait for another day if my sketch wasn't good enough to use as a basis for a painting later.

However, I didn't want to engage with him that much. No, I didn't fill him in on the fact I had the ability to make this whole chat so much easier for him. I'd lived in Europe long enough that I'd become fluent in French, Spanish, and Italian. Plus, my German and Greek were passable. No, this, whatever it was, would go much faster if I let him stumble along in a language he wasn't good at. He'd get frustrated and give up in a hot minute.

"Do you not want me to do my artwork in your church anymore?" I couldn't think of any other reason for him needing this little tete-a-tete.

"No, no. Art good, art gift God send." He paused, searching for something, the right word or phrase. "I worry you need thing. You come much. You sit. You no move long time. What you need?"

Here was yet another person insisting that my ability had nothing to do with my hard work. First Nikos, now this Father Antonio wanted me to doubt my own talent. I remained rather sure they were wrong on that score. I'd done the time, all of those countless hours of putting pen, pencil, brush to paper or canvas. Working hard over the years to perfect my craft, through trial and error. If Pat hadn't put a sketchbook into my hands, no way would I have ever done those first few crude drawings. My work was mine. Not this God as they so claimed.

As I contemplated how best to respond to the God issue, two cups of café con leche and a few pastries arrived. I debated about taking a few sips of my drink, milk tended to be something I avoided. Sugary treats as well. In the end, I refrained from allowing myself either indulgence. This God thing also appeared to be another luxury I couldn't afford. To believe in something outside of myself, to admit I needed anyone or anything. To leave myself vulnerable and at the mercy of someone else.

I knew where doing that led.

Watching the others around me rather than my host, I eyed those around us. Young people enjoying their morning chats. Lovers sneaking a kiss or two, friends giggling, others futzing with their phones. Normal morning anywhere on the planet where people maintained bonds with others.

Unlike me.

Which brought me to the other point he'd made, did I need anything? Don't think anyone had ever asked me that. Even wondered about that. Or considered that I might, in fact, not have everything. No, most people took from me and then came back asking for more.

They took my art pieces of course, and for that I had been paid handsomely over the years. But various people had also taken my dignity, my sense of self, my sense of value, my sense of being loved.

Worst of all, they'd taken my child.

Thus, on the face of it, the answer might appear to be simple, because I didn't have a home or a family, this is what I needed. I earned enough now that I no longer scraped by financially. No more trying to find apartments with a bunch of roommates for next to nothing. But by not having that type of living situation, I no longer had any ties to the world. On one level it had become easier for me, I no longer had to put up a false front for those I lived with. On another it was harder, isolation came at a high cost.

Yes, I now could afford to stay at luxury resorts if I so wished. But there wasn't anything that made somewhere 'home' in the places where I might choose to sleep for a night or two. There wasn't anyone giggling in the common living room when I would enter. No chipped coffee mugs with stains. No bras left on the shower hook from the other women. No scents of perfume in the hall. No fresh bread on the counter.

Still, I chose to live alone and separate once I had the funds to do so. I wandered from hotel to hostel to pension, everything I owned fit in two suitcases, give or take. Yes, this is the life I'd decided all of those years ago would be best for me. I might've taken another path at any point along the road. Tried to connect with others, forge bonds. Find a way to stay in one place for more than a hot minute.

Yet, somehow I never did. I remained untethered, unconnected, walled up in a prison for one.

However, something more remained missing in my life. Something that I couldn't quite put a finger on. Yet this elusive thing had to be the reason for so many sleepless nights. And why I still roamed, unable to plant myself. Why I didn't bother to find a way to create a link to anything or anyone.

Again, my silence created a conversation gap that couldn't be left unfilled, "You no family?"

I shifted my gaze towards him, what business was that of his? But his round face showed nothing but kindness and concern. "I'm alone in the world and have been for most of my adult life."

For a moment a flash of pain came over his face, "No." Again, his mind scrambled for the right word in English. "Adopt by God. Jesus give gift. Make us family." He waved his arm with a flourish over the whole crowd around us on the small terrace. A small grin on his face as his eyes crinkled.

Adoption. It's what robbed me of my child. It's what gave another woman an opportunity to have a family and made me childless. It's what started this journey of mine. I wasn't sure I could see that as a good thing. Not to mention, my own mixed-up family had been a disaster. Why would anyone want to believe that everyone is family?

No, family couldn't be anything good no matter how you viewed it.

About then, a memory from my hippy days jiggled loose. So many of them used to spout words about how much of a 'family' we were. Until the shit hit the fan and everyone would scatter. Thus, whether you were born into it or created it, there wasn't any way to make a family work. Yes, my viewpoint had become jaded and cynical over the years, colored by too many bad memories.

Therefore, in my experience, being a lone wolf had been the safer path to take. In my little bubble, there were no family or friends to speak of. And the only hurts and wounds I had were old, scarred over, buried deep. No new ones could be added because I'd been keeping people at arms length for something like forty years. With a few exceptions, like Nikos. Without me saying a word, I had no doubt all of these thoughts were written on my face. Not for Father Antonio's eyes, but for all the world to see right at that moment.

He patted my hand, "Family hurt. Much pain in you. I sorry."

Then another image flashed in my mind, of Stan as a toddler cowering under the kitchen table. Rather odd that, I don't believe I'd given him a second thought after I'd run away – over fifty years ago. While we only shared a Mother, we were still related, still family. Had he survived? Managed to come out of the wreckage and live an average to middling existence? Had he married, did he have kids? Had he turned into the same kind of monster his father was? Why had I never once tried to find him?

That answer was obvious, because the road to Stan led through my mother.

"Life isn't for the weak," I mumbled, a lame cliché but that remained the best I could do at the moment.

"God give no more we hold." He squeezed my hand so hard it hurt, then laid my hands open on the table. He placed a few objects from the table in one of my open palms, a napkin, a fork, a salt shaker. Then he raised it up, "You see? Make strong."

No, I didn't understand. All of my suffering had been heaped upon me because I had been capable of handling it? What kind of twisted logic did this guy believe? I narrowed my eyes, giving him a hard look.

"God hold you." He wrapped his fingers around mine.

"Well, maybe if I thought there was a God out there somewhere. But I don't." I pulled my hands back, scattering the items across the table.

"You con God." He hooked a thumb over his shoulder, pointing back towards the church we'd left a few moments before. "God bless, give art."

"Just because I hang out in churches all the time doesn't mean I'm doing anything even sort of religious." I snapped back, sliding my chair an inch or two away from the table. The time had come to exit this conversation, and this part of Spain. "God hasn't given me anything."

"Peace." He tapped a slim finger on the table, knowing one word was all he needed to say.

I leaned back into the table, propping my chin on my hand, tapping on the side of my cup. Yes, this is what I needed to find, a place where the universe found a small measure of harmony with my aching heart. Why I came back to sanctuaries of all types over and over again.

And it had nothing to do with my work as I pretended to be the case.

They remained the only place I could relax. Not have the constant and relentless tug of restlessness. Forever pulling me onward to the unknown. Within the walls of any church, chapel, whatever, I sensed something different. That presence sitting beside me, comforting me. Something holding me together after everything had fallen apart. But there had to be another reason for that besides a God or heavenly being.

But deep inside me I knew there could be no other answer.

I stared into the eddy I created as I swirled a spoon around the coffee, no beginning and no end. A yearning deep in my heart called to me. Those million times I'd told myself I didn't have a place I'd come from or a place I could go home to, were wrong. I in fact did. The time had come for me to reach out, and try again to have a conversation with my mother, Sharon.

The question remained, would she welcome me?

My last phone call with my mother led me to believe she never wanted me back, not in a million years. However, so much had changed as time had marched on. For me, and hopefully for her. And by now, Stan, my half-brother, would be his own man. We also needed to have a conversation. If for no other reason than to find a bit of closure. For he, as a small child, couldn't possibly have understood why I'd disappeared. But he wasn't my main focus, my mother was.

I needed to tell her I forgive her for not letting me come home when I was pregnant. My mistakes were mine, not hers. I also needed to tell her I understood a bit of what she'd dealt with, before Charles and because of Charles. And I wanted to help her escape him if she hadn't already. Because no woman should be in that kind of situation.

But most of all, my mother should be given what I'd received. Peace. At the end of the day, it didn't matter what she did or didn't do. How great of a Mother she was or wasn't. She should have this gift I'd found. Even if I couldn't quite comprehend what all I'd learned and discovered, it was real. And I needed to help her find a small measure of the contentment I now had.

"I'm sure you're not going to understand this, but I think I need to find my mother. Tell her I get it now, her life, her dark path, my place in her world." I gave him a sideways glance to gauge his reaction.

"Is good." He, calm as could be, took a bite of a croissant. Like this conversation wasn't anything special or earth shattering.

I, however, understood how profound a shift I'd just made.

<h1 style="text-align:center">CHAPTER 21</h1>

<h1 style="text-align:center">New Mexico – Present Day</h1>

W e'd reached the small stream and had stopped to rest on the small iron bench beside it. The tall aspen trees provided a small amount of shade though they'd shed half their fall leaves already. The cool breeze wafting over us was as refreshing as the icy water from the spring we were now sipping from. An idyllic little hollow. The granite rocks worn from decades of cascading water rushing over them. The forested mountains sloping up behind.

"And that's when you reconnected with your brother?" Timothy had a skeptical look on his face, "No way it was that easy. And what about your mother?"

It hadn't been.

I didn't wish to have more than one visit with my mother unless absolutely necessary. I'd flown into New York a few weeks after my chat with Father Antonio. Once there, I used the library to conduct research. In less than an hour, I'd discovered she'd been beaten to death by Charles in the late 70s. Part of me wept, compelled to experience some measure of sadness. Part of me sighed a deep sigh of relief, the hard conversation wouldn't ever happen.

I'd both dreaded and anxiously anticipated our reunion, unsure how it would play out. Now I'd never be given the chance to say my peace, never know if I might have been able to help. And I did wonder what would have happened if I had reached out when I first started to make a bit of money. Would I have been able to change the outcome in the end? Would she have accepted my offer of help? Would she have left Charles before it was too late?

Another one of those might have been added to a very long list.

After a few moments of hesitation, I made the decision to press on with my task. There remained one more person to find even if he hadn't been my priority to begin with. It took me a bit more to find an obituary of people I believed to be Stan's grandparents, Charles's parents. They'd apparently raised Stan after Charles had gone to prison. And from there a possibility of where Stan might be. The internet is a wonderful thing. Yes, it'd been possible to do all of this while still in Europe. But I'd wanted to be able to be close enough to act on whatever information I might learn.

Before I chickened out.

"A few false starts, but in the end, I did manage it. I think, all things considered, he's an okay guy. Got a couple of kids, a few grandkids. Nice, safe, boring life somewhere. Not sure he appreciated me dropping into his world. And now that my daughter keeps calling him," I gripped the cold armrest as I conjured up the one image I had of Stan. "Well, he might just stop talking to me. As for my mother, she passed away shortly after I arrived in Europe." I didn't see any reason to darken the moment with the truth of the matter.

As for the reunion with Stan, we'd met at a diner for supper in his hometown in California. I'd flown across the country just for those few precious minutes. Even so, me being a stranger and all, I wasn't fit to invite to a meal at his house with the family. His soft blue button-down shirt, dark blue tie, pressed gray slacks, brown loafers screamed uptight. Everything about him was all too formal for the setting. I wore my typical flowing flowery type dress, with sandals. Easy-breezy, comfortable. We chit-chatted about everything and nothing. The evening ended with him saying he forgave me for leaving him behind. For allowing him to witness our mother be murdered at the hands of his father. For not showing up for her funeral. Or not being there for any of the other important things in his life.

Like I had much of a choice at the time. But thanks for laying all of that guilt at my feet.

Neither of us left that conversation knowing anything substantial about each other. We emailed, called on the important dates, nothing more. Yet this fragile bond held somehow. Initially, I'd stayed in America with the idea I'd visit him again. Thinking maybe in a year I'd go back to my old habits and haunts in Europe. Thus, I'd found this listing for an idyllic rustic cabin in the mountains of New Mexico. Two states away from where he lived. Close enough to visit, not near enough to appear to be stalking him. However, in 2020 the world had other plans for my life and for everyone else's.

And here I still remained.

"Why doesn't he just give your daughter your number?" Timothy tapped a finger on his lips. "You're the older sister, right?"

This hadn't ever crossed my mind. Why did Stan believe he needed to be the gatekeeper? What did I need protection from? "Maybe he knows more about me than he's letting on."

"That call you made to your mother?" He looked up at the clouds floating across the sky, as intangible as this whole idea. "When you were pregnant..."

"How would he know about that? He was just a kid." My mind tried to think of other possibilities. Several scenarios sprang up. Drunken utterances in the heat of an argument being the most likely.

My mother hadn't been one to hold secrets, and she and Charles drank from morning till night from what I could tell. Yet, that might explain why he'd kept me at arm's length. He thought he'd been told everything important about me already before I'd found him. But goodness only knew what he'd heard over the years about his wayward sister. "Never mind, I think I can work that answer out." Heaving a massive sigh, I grimaced.

Time to call Stan.

"Got your phone on ya?" Timothy nodded his chin my way. "Cuz, Miss Donna, I enjoy chatting with you and all. But from the sounds of it, you should be having this conversation with someone else."

Impertinent brat! Fine, I'd been thinking along the same lines, however he didn't need to spell it out for me. "Of course not, the cord isn't that long." I snorted, trying not to laugh.

"Wait, the only phone you use is the one in the cabin?" The raised eyebrows, wide open eyes, agape mouth said it all. I'm a troglodyte. Stuck in the past, unable and unwilling to move forward.

I gave a slight shrug, not wishing to give any additional information that would make me appear even worse. I also didn't have a tablet which everyone else on the planet seemed to have. Plus, my laptop is so old it was used when I bought it at a pawnshop when I first came back to the states. I only got the stupid thing because I knew that America isn't like Europe, there's no corner bakery everywhere. I'd have to use the internet to order stuff. Plus, I'd have to have my own way of checking my email since there's no internet cafes here either.

And I hadn't turned the T.V. in the cabin on even once, don't ask me what the most popular show is. Famous artists I can tell you everything about. Famous actors not so much. My life remained stuck firmly in the past in so many ways. I didn't vote. I didn't watch the news. I didn't listen to popular music.

And of course there was the beat-up, worn-out faded blue Bug I'd shown up in. It had been thirty years old the day I first drove it off the lot in New Jersey in 2019. I'd bought it at a junkyard no less. Yes, I could've afforded a new car, and the most expensive one on the market. But I didn't understand the technology in them. I went to one dealership and the guy started talking about keyless this. And push button start that, bluetooth something. I left completely bewildered, befuddled, frustrated. At the junkyard, the guy helped me replace a few parts in it so it'd run sorta okay and I was good to go. No muss, no fuss.

Repairing beat up VW Bugs was one of the many things I'd learned to do in the 70s.

"Don't suppose you're the one person on the planet who happens to remember phone numbers still." He shifted a bit as he removed his tiny, slim phone from his back pocket. The little wonder he'd managed to access the internet from earlier, don't have a clue how these kids did that.

"Since the only number I ever call is Stan's, that's easy." I gazed down at the object he held out to me. As I reached out to accept it, Timothy started to rise, "No, stay. This will be a rather short call and it's cool for you to be here. I only need to ask how to reach my daughter. Do think it's best if we have this conversation in person, I'm no good with speaking on phones. You can't figure out body language that way."

He hesitated, floating an inch or so above the bench for a moment before settling back down. Good thing he did, in the end, I needed his assistance to use the darn thing. There didn't seem to be any buttons to push.

Stan let the call go to voicemail, guess since he didn't recognize the number, he didn't see the need to answer it. "Hey, it's Donna, how do I get in touch with this woman, er, my daughter? Ya know, the person you said keeps calling, Jenny? Oh, okay, call me back. Wait, Timothy, what's the number?"

"He'll know, it shows up on most systems." He pointed towards the phone, but I guess I threw him some weird look because he did spit out the digits as well.

A second later Stan called back. "Hey sis. She said she's on her way to Texas, she'll be there in a few days. Which is really close to you. Here's her number and her email address." He blabbed out the numbers and the Gmail account.

"Thanks, I don't have a pen on me, can you email that to me in case I forget that?" I gulped. "And just so you are aware, I want to tell you the whole story about her someday soon. I'll come visit. Or not. Only if it's okay by you. Let me know. If you don't want me to, then forget it. Right? Sorry, forget I even mentioned it."

"It's fine, Donna. I'd like that, to see you that is. We should've had more than that one visit. You need to meet your family." He hung up without adding anything more.

Texas? Why there? I scratched the corner of my eye. Then the answer hit me like a ton of bricks. Duh, I felt so stupid right at that second. She'd already found Bruce.

"Hey, you don't look so good. You're whiter than a ghost. Do you want me to go get you some more water?" He tapped on my hand that rested on my lap.

"Jenny's going to meet her father." The man I'd forced into a situation he hadn't been mature enough to deal with. I hadn't given him more than a few passing thoughts over the years. At one time I'd believed he would be the one man who wouldn't fail me, who would protect me in the end. But I wasn't destined to be the type of woman you take home to meet your mother.

"Are you good with that?" He rocked forward for a moment, trying to better read the expression on my face.

I twisted my lip, curling it inward to gnaw on it as I debated this whole idea for a second or two. Bruce and I ended badly, no way around that. We needed closure. Our child needed to learn who she is, or why else would she be trying to find us. Thus, the time had come to bring this full circle.

For all three of us.

"Yes, I do believe I am. I need to go to Texas." Standing up, a new sense of purpose filled me as I began to march back towards the resort.

"And I have to call the agency and tell them I want to try to connect with my birth Mother." Timothy called out from behind me.

"Good for you!" Stopping for a second, I whipped around and gave him a gentle squeeze on the shoulder.

When we neared our respective homes, we parted ways. As I entered my tiny space, I headed straight for my laptop resting on the counter in the kitchen area. Flipping open the clunky lid, I stood before it. Bouncing on the balls of my feet, I debated what to say to this unknown child of mine.

Jenny,

    Thank you for wanting to connect. This is rather difficult for me for many reasons. I'm sorry that I didn't respond the first few times that Stan told me you had reached out. However, I'll be heading out for Texas tomorrow and will call you when I arrive. I don't have a cell phone, but you can email me back or wait for me to tell you what hotel I'll be staying in.

    I'm sorry for everything. I'm sorry I couldn't be your mother. I'm sorry I never even knew if you were a boy or a girl. I'm sorry if I have caused you any pain or if you had to live a life full of questions. I'm sorry if you don't understand any of this.

    I hope you had a good life. I hope you had a wonderful, kind mother who gave you everything I never could. I hope you had a strong, patient father who stood beside you for everything.

    I think I'm ready to meet you, to tell you anything you need to know, to give you a sense of where you come from. To fill you in on where I've been your entire life.

Donna

I scanned over it several times, something about it didn't have the right vibe but I couldn't put my finger on what. Before I could change my mind, I hit send. By now the afternoon sun had moved well past the middle of my living room, dinner time would be arriving soon. Yet my stomach wasn't growling with hunger, rather it leaned toward the queasy side. Closing the laptop lid with a swift and sure movement, I glided into my bedroom. Scanning the room for a moment, I began to stuff things into my suitcases. I'd doubted I'd be returning to this place, I'd have to double check it to ensure nothing was left behind.

As I finished taking the last load to the car, I looked around the cabin. The lone item left I'd placed on the counter with a note for Tim. I'd taken about an hour in my frantic push to leave to finish the piece he'd admired earlier in the day. Now it would be his, to cherish or to sell to fund his future. Despite the late hour, a deep desire to start the journey filled me with a sense of urgency. Leaving me not wanting to wait until the morning. Closing the door, my heart ached at leaving my home behind. For this truly had become my home over the last few years. Deep in my heart, I regretted not getting to know Tim better during that time. We were more alike than I'd ever imagined, and in one short day we'd become friends.

It was now time to face my past.

About the Author

Leigh Lincoln is an author whose narratives resonate deeply with the human experience. With a passion for storytelling that touches hearts and provokes thoughtful reflection, she has carved a path that intertwines her love for writing with her dedication to advocating for the homeless and those living in poverty. Her journey as an author is a testament to her commitment to making people ponder the choices they make, how they treat others, and the importance of empathy. Leigh's journey has led her down a remarkable path of advocacy for the homeless and impoverished communities. For over three decades, she has dedicated herself to making a difference in the lives of those in need. Her first novel, "Road Home," was born from this tireless work. It serves as a thought-provoking mirror to society, challenging readers to consider how they live, treat others, and desire to be treated.

Leigh's most recent series, "Path to Family," is her most personal work to date. These novels will shine a light on the emotional and hopeful tale of adoption from the perspectives of those involved. Through this series, Leigh shares her own deeply personal adoption experience with her readers, inviting them to connect with the emotional depths of the narrative.

You can connect with Leigh by signing up for her newsletter at: https://leighlincolnauthor.com/subscribe/
You will receive a free short story and occasional updates on her life, travels, and upcoming novels.